If These WALLS *Could* TALK:
BOSTON RED SOX

If These WALLS Could TALK:
BOSTON RED SOX

Stories from the Boston Red Sox Dugout, Locker Room, and Press Box

Jerry Remy and Nick Cafardo

30 YEARS
TRIUMPH
BOOKS

Library of Congress Cataloging-in-Publication Data

Names: Remy, Jerry, 1952– author. | Cafardo, Nick., co-author.
Title: If these walls could talk : Boston Red Sox : stories from the Boston
   Red Sox dugout, locker room, and press box / Jerry Remy and Nick Cafardo.
Description: Chicago, Illinois : Triumph Books LLC, [2019]
Identifiers: LCCN 2019005303 | ISBN 9781629375458
Subjects: LCSH: Boston Red Sox (Baseball team)—History. | Boston Red Sox
   (Baseball team)—Anecdotes.
Classification: LCC GV875.B62 R459 2019 | DDC 796.357/640974461—
dc23 LC record available at https://lccn.loc.gov/2019005303

This book is available in quantity at special discounts for your group or organization. For further information, contact:
   Triumph Books LLC
   814 North Franklin Street
   Chicago, Illinois 60610
   (312) 337–0747
   www.triumphbooks.com

Printed in U.S.A.
ISBN: 978-1-62937-545-8
Design by Amy Carter
Page production by Patricia Frey

To my grandchildren, Dominik and Arianna, whom I love more than anything in this world. They are the joy of my life and give me incredible strength and courage.

—J.R.

CONTENTS

FOREWORD

Over the 35 years since I graduated from Syracuse (aka "The Harvard of Central New York") and embarked on a career in sports broadcasting, I have kept a list of the names of every analyst, producer, director, sideline reporter, and studio host with whom I have worked on the local and national level. In the four major sports alone, the number of different color commentators is 104 (baseball 30, football 25, basketball 35, and hockey 14). When you add golf, tennis, soccer, lacrosse, bobsled, and luge, the number is more than 160. Some were much more talented than others. Some were much easier to be around than others. With very few exceptions (and the list of names of the "exceptions" will wait for my book), I have enjoyed working with each of them. But the pairing I will always view as special, and unique, is my nine-year partnership with Jerry Remy in the Red Sox television booth.

Jerry and I started in the Red Sox booth, though not together, in 1988. I was paired alongside long-time analyst and former Red Sox catcher Bob Montgomery in the WSBK-TV38 booth. Jerry joined Red Sox legend Ned Martin on the NESN cablecasts. For me, at age 25, it was the fulfillment of my childhood dream and an opportunity I embraced with tremendous excitement and gratitude. For Jerry, not far removed from a major league playing career, it was a way to stay in the game and continue to make a living. I got the sense it was an opportunity he undertook with great trepidation about whether or not he would be able to do the job.

I worked with Monty for eight years. During that time, I got to know Jerry as we traveled together on the road with the Red Sox. I didn't know him well. By his own admission, very few people know Jerry well. But as I listened to him talk and tell stories on buses and airplanes, and in restaurants and hotels, I knew that I liked him. And I was convinced that there was much more to his personality, and his broadcasting ability, that had not come out to the NESN audience.

Starting with the 1996 season, the "over-the-air" telecasts moved to WABU-TV, and its station management, in conjunction with the Red Sox and NESN, decided that Jerry would be the analyst on all of the TV games. While I felt bad for Monty, who was losing a job that he enjoyed and at which he worked hard, I was excited for the opportunity to work with Jerry.

I did not consciously enter into this new partnership with the goal of dragging out more of Jerry's personality, in part because I didn't know if he would be comfortable going there. But I knew that I would continue to do what I had always done, which is to engage the analyst in conversation (a must on baseball broadcasts during which there is so much "dead time" between pitches) and to ask the questions I think the viewers are asking as they watch. I didn't know how Jerry would respond, but I was hopeful and optimistic that the viewers and I would see more of the Jerry I had seen off the air. It didn't take long before we did.

Perhaps because we had spent eight years around each other, and respected and liked each other before we ever sat in a booth together, our strong on-air chemistry and rapport developed quickly. I think Jerry knew and trusted that I had his best interests at heart. If need be, I wanted to help lead him into conversations about game strategy, individual player skill, lessons learned from his own playing days, and anything else that might be appropriate given the game situation we were watching and analyzing. And when the game got one-sided and the audience wasn't hanging on every pitch, I hoped that Jerry would join me in trying to keep it interesting and fun by talking about other things that sometimes had little or nothing to do with what was happening on the field. Boy, did he ever.

These became some of my favorite moments, and now memories, of our time together. I believe that most, but not all, of our viewers enjoyed them, too. For Jerry and me, they came to be known as "Inane Banter." We had received a letter from an angry woman who implored us to "stick to the game" and let us know very clearly that she hated it when we drifted off into our "inane banter." I read her letter on the air and, from that point forward until the joke got old, we would warn the author of the letter that we were about to go off on a tangent by flashing an "Inane Banter Warning" graphic in the corner of the screen. It was in those moments when Jerry's personality came shining through, and Red Sox Nation began to see the sense of humor and storytelling ability that would play a big part in his becoming a Red Sox legend. As Jerry grew comfortable sharing more of himself, the moments happened more often. From his updates on *Days of Our Lives* to the emergence of his close friendship with "Wally the Green Monster," it was impossible to predict where Jerry might take us. But Red Sox Nation discovered that Jerry was interesting and funny, and we wanted more.

One of my goals was to make Jerry laugh so hard that he would take his headset off, or at least depress the "cough button" that would kill his microphone. There were many instances when that happened, or that he said something so funny that I, or both of us, went several pitches without saying anything. I remember our fantastic, and exasperated, producer Russ Kenn saying, "This is really professional, guys" in our ears after we killed our mics and laughed as the audience heard nothing from us while several pitches passed by. Often, we just went ahead and laughed, snorted, or snickered on the air. Is there a laugh that is better known in New England than Jerry's?

One night, we were in Cleveland as the Red Sox were playing the Indians. Justin Speier, a relief pitcher, came into the game for the Tribe. As I thumbed through the Indians media guide, I noticed that Speier had pitched collegiately at Nicholls State in Louisiana. I knew more than I should about Nicholls State, because its basketball team had played in an NCAA tournament game I called for CBS. So, I told Jerry, and our audience, that Nicholls State was named after Francis

T. Nicholls, a brigadier general in the Civil War who lost his left arm and foot in battle. When I mentioned that Nicholls returned to Louisiana to run for governor using the slogan "Vote for the REST of Me," Jerry lunged for the cough button. When I offered my opinion that this was probably a better slogan option than "I would give an arm and a leg to be governor," Jerry just about fired his headset off the wall. There was a long stretch during which neither of us said a word. (Additional historical footnote: the slogan was successful as Nicholls was twice elected governor of his home state.)

One night, at Fenway Park, we had an in-game visit from Judith Sheindlin, better known as "Judge Judy," whose popular arbitration-based courtroom reality show aired on our station and made her one of the highest-paid people in the history of American television. We had a nice on-air chat. It was in what transpired immediately after that visit where Jerry's ability to be funny spontaneously was on full display. After Judy and her grandsons left our booth and returned to their seats, we were informed by highly reputable booth personnel that the famed jurist and her grandsons departed our booth with a box of our Dunkin Donuts. Our crew took a shot of Judy and the boys, which presented clear video evidence that they were eating from a box of Dunkin Donuts that we, and our unimpeachable eyewitnesses who watched them abscond with the delectable treats from the booth, considered "stolen." A hilarious (at least to Jerry and me) conversation, that was clearly not intended to be taken seriously, about the possibility of legal action against America's best-known judge, ensued. It was relayed to us that Judy's "defense" was that she had asked if she could take the Dunkin Donuts before removing them from the booth. We were also told that the judge was none too pleased about our "false accusations." (Who knew, by watching her show, that Judy had a temper?) Anyway, we were pretty sure our evidence, and the testimony of our eyewitnesses/audio engineers/stage managers, would have held up in any court of law, including our personal favorite, *The People's Court*, in front of the all-time greatest TV Judge, the late, great Joe Wapner. But, fearful of a countersuit by Judy for trivial things like slander/libel/damage to reputation, etc., Jerry and I offered a completely sincere on-air apology to Judge Judy. At least, that's how I recall it. Now, fearful that the statute of limitations might not have run out, I offer another equally sincere apology, on behalf of Jerry and me, on these pages. Part of the appeal of Jerry's humor is that he is not afraid to press the boundaries of appropriateness and is not impacted by the threat of inadvertently offending someone (or of legal action), as the previous examples demonstrate (although I deserve any blame for inappropriateness relative to Gov. Nicholls).

This is also a huge part of Jerry's popularity as a baseball analyst. And it is his skill as a baseball broadcaster, even more than his likeable and diverse personality, that contributed most to his well-deserved reputation, both in New England and nationally. He is as well liked (and by many of his legion of fans, loved) and respected as any baseball analyst in America during his time. I know it is a big statement, and I promise you I don't make it lightly. I make it with tremendous appreciation of the many talented men and women who have delighted their viewers with their insights and personalities in MLB booths across North America over the past four decades. None has entertained *and* educated their viewers more than Jerry Remy.

The most important part of a broadcaster's job is the preparation that goes into each broadcast. Jerry was as well prepared as any of the analysts I have worked with in any sport. He arrived to the park ridiculously early to gather as much information as he could from as many sources as possible. He was in the clubhouse before most of the players had arrived. He was plugged into everything that was going on with the ballclub, on the field and behind the scenes. In this way, he reminded me of my father, the late, great *Boston Globe* sportswriter Will McDonough. People confided in him because they trusted him and knew that their trust would not be violated. It is the key to being a great reporter. And Jerry is a great reporter. He knows what he can say on the air and what is to stay between him and those who give him sensitive information. All of the information is helpful to a broadcaster, even if he can't use it on the air. Jerry knows if the pitcher doesn't like a certain catcher, or if the manager thinks a player isn't very good and wants someone else called up from the minors, or if a pitcher isn't going to throw one of the pitches in his repertoire because he is hurt or because the pitch has lost its effectiveness. He might be able to pass it along to his audience. Or perhaps he cannot. But he knows what most other people don't know. And it is a part of what makes him great.

He also has tremendous baseball knowledge *and* the ability to express it. He is not reluctant to question decisions made by the Red Sox manager, or the performance of the players and front office. He knows how to do it in a respectful and appropriate manner. His allegiance is to his audience, but he is also part of a team, and when you work for NESN, you, by extension, work for the team. He walks that tightrope very well. He wouldn't be around for four decades if he did not. His ability to anticipate and analyze game situations, his high baseball IQ, and his personality would combine to make a top-shelf analyst. To me, he took a step to a level occupied by very few when he got comfortable on television and with television.

When his career began, he would watch the game and respond to the action as, or after, it unfolded. As the years passed, he learned to use the medium to help him anticipate, analyze, and teach. We have a "talkback button" attached to our headsets. We use it to speak with the producer and director without it going on the air. Jerry learned what a valuable tool this can be. Rather than just watching the game and reacting, Jerry would use the talkback to request shots of players playing too close/far from the line, outfielders who are too shallow or deep, batters who are too far/close to the plate, pitchers at one end of the rubber or the other, the grip pitchers use to throw pitches and how they might be tipping them, and anything else that got his attention as he looked down on the field. He anticipated situations rather than just reacting to them. When Jerry got comfortable with letting more of himself come through to his audience, and when he got more comfortable with being on television and with how to use television, he became a complete broadcaster, a New England legend, and one of the great baseball analysts of all time, anywhere in the country.

He is known to many as the "RemDawg," a nickname that I gave him early in our time together. It was at a time when the word "dawg" had become particularly trendy. "What up, dawg?" was a frequently asked question. I believe it was also around the same point when the Red Sox players became known as the "Dirt Dogs" for their gritty style. To me, "gritty" is a good word to describe Jerry's style. He was a creature of habit as a player and that carries into his personal and professional life. Jerry leaves for the park at the same time every day, heads down to the clubhouse at the same time, fills out his lineup card at the same time, and eats his pregame meal at the same time. He takes his job very seriously and works very hard at it. There was just something about "RemDawg" that seemed to fit the man and the times. I don't remember the first time I called him by that nickname, but it stuck and spread—a part of his legacy and Red Sox lore. Jerry has always been extremely gracious in giving me credit for helping bring out his personality. I don't deserve it. I might have prodded and encouraged, but he is the one who had to live it and do it. And while I am delighted that Jerry has made a lot of money off "RemDawg" T-shirts, hats, mugs, scorecards, and whatever else he could find a way to sell, in lieu of giving me credit for giving him the nickname, he can send me 10 percent of all "RemDawg" merchandise sold.

The "RemDawg" is not a character, but in many ways, Jerry Remy is a different person on air than he is off air. That is not in any way to suggest that he is a fraud in either area. Off the air, Jerry is not social. That is the biggest reason why he and I spent very little time together off the air. In fact, I think it is fair to describe him as socially awkward. I know people who have met him in person who thought he was unfriendly and aloof. He is not. But he is not comfortable around people he does not know. People see Jerry's personality through the television. They understand his humor, they appreciate his ability to make fun of himself, they can tell he is a good person. Perhaps because he is speaking into a microphone and looking into a camera but can't see the people to whom he is speaking, he is comfortable interacting with the world in that way. Most of the analysts I know who have become extremely popular, in large part because of their personality, are big personalities and gregarious on and off the air; people like Bill Raftery, Dick Vitale, and Charles Barkley, to name a few. Jerry is not that person, which makes his extraordinary popularity even that much more remarkable to me.

And, finally, I want you to know that Jerry Remy is a good person. He has his quirks (we had to be out of the booth 10 seconds after we signed off the air or else he was visibly annoyed and anxious, leading me to ask if I could please have just a few seconds to put my stuff in my bag), and I did not enjoy being around his smoking (even then, he was courteous, walking to the back of the booth or setting up a fan to blow the smoke out the window). But I never remember a truly unpleasant exchange, on or off the air. Jerry is one of those people who doesn't reach out much, but who always does when it is important. When my dad died, when I left the Red Sox, when I was hired for and when I left *Monday Night Football*, and on many other important occasions in my life, Jerry has always been there for me. And I hope he feels that I have always been there for him, because he has certainly had more health challenges and unspeakable tragedy to deal with than anyone I know.

I have gone on way longer than I intended (Jerry will not be surprised by this). But then again, there are many facets to Jerry's life. He has experienced the extreme ends of the spectrum—from total joy and exhilaration to tragedy that is impossible to comprehend. And so much in between. Of all of the sports, baseball announcers are the most popular (Vin Scully, Harry Caray, Jack Buck, Bob Uecker, and Ernie Harwell are just a few examples) because we listen to them every night and we feel that we know them. We get a window into who they are. It was part of the reason why Jerry received such an amazing outpouring of support as he revealed his battles with cancer and depression. People truly care about Jerry. And it is why the Red Sox, NESN, and most of Red Sox Nation stood by him in the wake of the unimaginably evil act carried out by his son Jared.

Given that he has grown so much more comfortable opening up to us over the years, I trust this book will be heartfelt and honest, even though parts of his story will be incredibly difficult to tell. He is a great storyteller. And a good man. We know that. He has demonstrated that to us on countless summer nights over dozens of baseball seasons when he brought so much happiness to so many. It is why fans like, or love, and respect him. It is why this friend and fan loves, likes, and respects him.

Sean McDonough was the television play-by-play announcer for the Boston Red Sox from 1988 to 2004, during which time he was honored four times with the New England Sports Emmy Award for Outstanding Play-by-Play. He is now a leading play-by-play commentator for ESPN college football and basketball games in addition to calling the annual Par 3 Contest at The Masters. Most recently the voice of Monday Night Football, McDonough has covered the World Series, NCAA Final Four, the Olympic Games, and all four major golf championships, among other marquee events during his accomplished career.

INTRODUCTION

So, how lucky am I?

Despite the health issues and the personal tragedies I've gone through in the past decade, my one refuge has been that I love broadcasting Red Sox games and have since this second career began back in 1988. I never thought I'd be any good at it and never had any desire to do it. I grew up listening to Ken Coleman and Ned Martin on TV and radio as a kid in Somerset, Massachusetts. I was fortunate to be good enough to be drafted by the California Angels and ultimately became a major-leaguer after a lot of hard work.

Growing up in Somerset, you don't really have an opportunity to play a lot of baseball because the weather in New England is so cold and rainy in the spring. It's more of a challenge for us to make it to the big leagues than a kid from Florida or California, Arizona or Texas. I knew I could run with anyone, steal bases, play good defense. I could hit. I had the red-ass as a player, so I was really intense on the field. The Angels were a great team to break in with but being traded to the Red Sox, my hometown team, before the 1978 season, was a dream come true. I'll get into that sometime later in this book as we rummage through the highlights of my playing career.

I have so many people to thank along the way who made both careers possible and who got the very best out of me, because at one time or another I probably wasn't very good at either one. I have so many people to thank for getting me through the toughest times in my life, the great fans who kept me going during the darkest days when at times I didn't have the will to live. The boxes of cards and letters and emails from so many people who cared about me, who said they missed me on the air in those times when I had to take a leave of absence while I was going through treatments. To survive all of that and come through it with the feeling that people really care has been one of the most humbling things I have ever experienced. I've tried to thank people on the air, through interviews, and now through this book, because it would be impossible to send a hand-written response to all of them. But rest assured, I've read everything ever sent to me.

With each health event I've had I know that I have had the best medical care in the world at Massachusetts General Hospital. My team of doctors have kept me positive and optimistic about my future. What also keeps me going is knowing I'll be back in the broadcast booth helping to analyze and dissect games for the viewers. And I must digress here and just say how incredibly supportive and patient my superiors at NESN have been through all of my absences. I also want to thank all the analysts who have filled in during my absence, and my broadcast partner, Dave O'Brien, who has had the tough task of working with multiple partners. I've had the best people to work for. Our boss at NESN, Sean McGrail, has been amazing and he's stuck with me, believing in me and my recovery and that Red Sox viewers want me back in the booth.

Red Sox management and ownership has been especially supportive, from John Henry and Tom Werner to Sam Kennedy. I received numerous calls and texts from them along the way. Even in the middle of their incredible postseason run in 2018, I would get an occasional text from Alex Cora, who must have had a thousand things on his mind, yet he took the time to send me short texts to let me know he was thinking of me. I remember former managers Terry Francona and John Farrell, who had his own bout with cancer, did the same. Werner, Henry, and Kennedy were unbelievable keeping in touch and making sure I was okay.

I appreciate the mentions by players and media and, well, it's brought me to tears at times, because in times like I've had, you really find out how people feel about you. The outpouring of support and love from this fan base, from this organization, has blown me away. I will never forget it.

By the end of the 2018 World Series, I couldn't wait to get back in the booth. Radiation has kicked me hard, but I learned to deal with it and learned that it takes time to regain your strength. There's nothing I can do to accelerate feeling 100 percent. By the time spring training rolls around, I was hoping to get some of my strength back to prepare for my next season. I planned on cutting back, maybe not taking as many road trips as I did in the past, but I'm sure not quitting because I love the job so much and I love being around this organization.

Since 2004, we've won four championships. We truly are the best team of this century and what I wasn't able to do as a Red Sox player—and I thought the 1978 team was going to be the team that did it—I've at least been able to experience up close and personal as a broadcaster.

So, let me tell you my story over the next couple hundred pages or so. There are many times I've laughed and so many times I've cried. But every day I thank the Good Lord that I'm a Boston Red Sox.

CHAPTER 1
THE BEGINNING

Our family moved from Fall River, Massachusetts, to Swansea, and then to Somerset around the time I was ready to play Little League. My dad, Joseph, and my mother, Connie, had wanted to leave the triple decker tenement we lived in in Fall River for some time and they finally scraped together enough money to purchase a very modest home in a working-class neighborhood— one that was best for my sister, Judy, and me to grow up in.

Little League baseball seemed to come pretty easy to me and I was like every good player at that age in that I played shortstop and I pitched. I was a terrible pitcher but a good left-handed hitter. I could tell—and all the coaches could tell—that there was something there a little bit different than the other kids. My team was the Orioles. I think the fact I was good got my mother interested in what I was doing with sports. My mother was a dance instructor and a hairdresser, and my father worked at Globe Manufacturing, a rubber plant in Fall River. We moved to Swansea first, where we had a very modest little home. Our home was just down the road from my mother's parents. My grandfather was a huge, huge Red Sox fan. And my father was a huge Ted Williams fan. So that's how I really got involved with the game of baseball. I could remember sitting with my grandfather. In those days most of the games were on radio. He'd sit out on his porch and he'd be smoking a big cigar while listening to the games. I'd sit there and listen to them with him. And he would just go absolutely bonkers when somebody would walk. He hated walks.

My mother knew nothing at all about baseball, but she probably became one of the biggest fans the Red Sox would ever have before she passed away. But she learned everything about the game through my father and through watching me. Our house in Somerset was a step above what we had in Swansea. And the location was ideal because I was only 50 feet away from a park, which had a baseball field, a basketball court, a softball field, and a little pond that used to freeze in the winter, so we were able to skate on it. I had all the sports right there for me to do all the time. And that's where I spent all of my free time. It was a great place to grow up because there were always kids at that playground doing something.

We had all these weird games where you had four guys on the field and one would be hitting, one would be pitching, one would be in the outfield, and one would be in the infield. And we just used half the field. If it was a right-handed hitter, everybody would play the left side. Because I was a left-handed hitter, they'd pitch to me from third base. If I'd pull the ball they wouldn't have to move. So, I'd hit it to that field.

I could hear my mother yell for me from the house when it was time to come home. It was that kind of a setup.

When I started playing organized baseball the coaches immediately made me the shortstop, which was usually the best player. I had my Yaz stance with the bat held high. Yaz was my hero. It was 1967 when I really took to listening and watching all the games. That team caught the attention of everybody in New England. I was lucky enough to watch what he did in '67 when he won the Triple Crown in one of the greatest seasons by any player in history. And then I got to play with him, which was pretty remarkable. Every time I played against him when I was with the Angels was pretty amazing.

But back in Little League, I know there were officials and coaches fighting over me. I don't know what the ins and outs were. I just know my coach was Pete Reese and that I always ended up on the Orioles. That was my first introduction to organized baseball. It was a ton of fun. Four years of Little League went by so fast. At that time, Little League was for kids nine to 12 years old. And those years just seemed to fly by.

My dad loved baseball and he played softball late in life, on nights and weekends when he was still working. He was a kind guy. After working at the manufacturing plant, he became a furniture salesman at Mason's Furniture in Fall River. His love for Ted Williams was off the charts. Everything Ted did, that's all he talked about. He loved horse racing and dog racing. He liked to play cards. And he would always try to get my mother to move to Florida, but she would have none of it until later on in life when they eventually wound up down there. If my mother said I was a bad boy one day, he was responsible for coming home and taking care of it with the strap. I think half the time he was using the strap on me he didn't know what I had done wrong. But he wasn't pushy, sports-wise. He just had a love for baseball and that love kind of trickled down to me. He taught me a lot about baseball, but I think I was more self-taught.

I used to pretend the back of my grandfather's house was the Green Monster. I used to throw the ball up by myself and then try to hit it off the Green Monster. It just so happened that right field was the longer part of the field, so I thought I was playing at Fenway. The roof itself was the screen at Fenway Park and the house was the left-field wall. It wasn't green. I think it was something like a pink house, some weird color. And I remember going out there and just throwing the Wiffle balls and tennis balls and whacking them off the house. Maybe that's how I got my opposite-field stroke. The problem is when I got to the big leagues I couldn't reach the left-field wall!

Those childhood days were special to me. There were no worries. There were no complications. It was just having fun. I had a good family. I felt loved. The atmosphere I grew up in is what I knew. My life was playing baseball and, later as a teenager, spending time with my friends, smoking Marlboros and drinking Buds.

Baseball was my first love. I loved all sports. When basketball season would come around, I'd play basketball. And then football. And flag football. But baseball was always the one I looked forward to, for some reason. Maybe it's because I felt I had some talent there. I don't know. I guess it was built into my family because of the way my father and my grandfather emphasized it and talked about it so much.

The one thing I always had going for me was that I was fast. I remember some fast kid from Somerset High wanted to race. We raced, and I think the kid beat me. And I couldn't believe it because nobody had ever beaten me before. I always had really good speed. That helped me in a lot of sports, especially in pickup basketball games, because although I couldn't shoot, I could drive by people. I was always the end in football because I could run the routes and beat everybody.

When I got to high school, my coach, Jim Sullivan, was the football and baseball coach. I wanted to play all three sports and I remember going out for football as a halfback. But I never made it into a game. I'll never forget the first time I carried the ball in practice. It was like a maze going through the line. I couldn't see where I was going. There were people all over the place trying to block. I can't be sure how many practices I made it through, but Coach Sullivan came up to me and he said, "Look, the wise thing for you to do would be to play baseball because there's no sense in you getting hurt playing football." So I left the team. I never played a snap of football in high school but I loved it as a kid growing up. But because of his advice and because I trusted him so much, I just focused on baseball.

I still wanted to keep playing basketball. I was playing on the JV team and I had an injury to my right hand, my shooting hand, and I didn't tell the coach. We got into a game and a pass came to me in the corner and I took a shot with my left hand. And he went ape shit. I mean he just went crazy. At halftime we got into the locker room and he just tore into me about shooting with my left hand. He said, "What are you doing?"

5

I said, "Well, my right hand is hurt."

He said, "Well, you've got to tell me." He was pissed. And so that was the end for me.

After he tore into me about that I said, "I'm not up for this."

Baseball then became everything to me. I was always trying to keep my grades up so I could make the baseball team. I was not a good student at all. My grades were sinking because I was doing all the other sports but I really wanted to play baseball, so I was really trying to do everything I possibly could to get the grades good enough to be able to be on the baseball team.

One of my best friends to this day is Henry Veloza. He was a great kid and although we don't talk as much as we used to, we're still in contact. We had some crazy times as high school kids, I'll tell ya. We were *this* far from being in trouble all the time. And another friend of mine was Bob Fortin, but he didn't go to Somerset High, he went to Bishop Connolly. But we were all really close and we raised some hell. How we didn't end up in jail at times, I don't know. I didn't put much focus on school. But we loved our sports and we loved to have a good time. Life goes on and you don't see these people as much as you used to. But the fact is they're always in your heart because they're part of your childhood.

What was really weird was when I was playing in high school they used to tell me scouts were there, but I never really saw any. There was one local scout from Fall River named Skippy Lewis, who worked for the Washington Senators. Coach Sullivan got his attention and asked him to watch me play. And he eventually drafted me to the Washington Senators in the 19th round of the June amateur draft in 1970. As a matter of fact, Ted Williams was the manager of the Senators at that time, which my dad loved. For me it was not even a question: I wanted to sign. And then I had other people saying I had to go to school and get a college education. Well, I wasn't a good student.

I finally made a decision, probably against my father's will, to try college. And the reason I tried college was because we had another kid in town, Chucky Souza, who was a very good player. He went to St. Leo's in Florida. And he was one of these big power hitters, a guy who could hit the ball off the school on the other side of the field. He was a couple of years older than me and he kind of talked me into going to St. Leo's to play college baseball. The thing is, I never got invited by St. Leo's to go down there. It was just his word to the coach that he knew a pretty good player up here in Somerset who might be a good player at St. Leo's. There was no money for me coming out of high school, so I went down to St. Leo's with Chucky. I remember getting to the first practice, but I never got into the locker room. The coach came walking out and he said to me, "I hate to tell you this, but you're academically ineligible to play." Back then anybody could get in there.

I said, "What!"

He said, "I suggest you go to a junior college for a couple of years and come back and play here." I knew right way that I would never do that.

I stayed down there for about two weeks and actually enrolled for classes, but I never bought a book. I played in ping-pong tournaments every day. I never did any work. I called my parents and told them I was coming home. Man, were they upset. I tried to explain to them what happened. I said I'm not going to a junior college in Florida. I don't know anything about Florida. I told them the only reason I came down was because Chucky told me that I'd probably be playing at St. Leo's. I don't know if the story about me being academically ineligible was correct or if the coach just didn't want me. I have no idea because he never saw me play.

I came back up north and enrolled at Roger Williams College in Providence, Rhode Island, and finished out a semester. My childhood friend Henry also went there, so we used to drive up together. In those days there was a secondary draft in January, and much to my surprise, the Angels picked me in the eighth round of the 1971 draft, even though I had never spoken to anybody from the Angels. I always had the feeling that I was one of those leftover players who didn't sign in the original draft and then got picked in the secondary draft. Even there I was a low pick.

The scout who signed me was Dick Winseck. I met him in Boston, but there was no real money involved. It was $500 a month to play rookie league ball and they also offered to pay for my college education for a couple of years, not knowing at the time that they were going to send me to winter ball every year and that I would never go to college. I really didn't give a shit. I remember being up there with my father and signing my first professional contract with this guy who I'd never met in my life. I don't know how they got the name, I don't know how they got the information. I never saw him at a game. To me it was like they looked at the draft list from June, looked at the guys who didn't sign, and they said, "Okay, let's try to sign a couple of these guys up." I was just a guy they took and that was it. There were no expectations at all. That's how I ended up with the Angels.

When I first got to the minors I was so outclassed. I'm playing with kids from California, Texas, and Florida. My high school schedule was 16 games and we got snowed out of two of those. I had basically no experience compared to the kids I was playing with. And when I got down there it was a real eye-opener to see how badly I was behind these kids. It was depressing because I was like, "What the hell am I doing here? I don't belong here." I made it through my first spring training and they were going to release me instead of going to what they called it in those days, the "short season." It was just

June, July, and August. I was in Holtville, California, down near the Mexican border. That's where the minor leagues trained. I heard the story later that in their meetings they were going to send me home. There was one guy who stood up for me—Kenny Myers. He was an old crusty baseball guy who had worked for the Dodgers for many, many years. He had turned Willie Davis into a good player. He liked me because I could run. He's the reason—the only reason—that my professional baseball career continued. He said, "If he can run, I can teach him how to play." And that's what he had done with Willie Davis.

I'll never forget that. I didn't know it at the time but the farm director, Tom Sommers, told me when I made the big leagues: "You were on your way home because nobody was behind you. We saw you, you were well behind. We didn't think you had the tools." I finally got to talk to Kenny—well, you didn't talk much to Kenny. Kenny did a lot of talking to you. He was like a roving instructor so if we had a 7:00 PM game he had me out there at 10:00 in the morning just working on hitting, working on everything. He was tough but he was a great teacher. He did teach me how to play professional baseball. It was tough, but it made me tough.

I was on the Idaho Falls team and they optioned me to a team in Twin Falls, Idaho. That was one of my first real challenges, being on a team my first year with a bunch of guys who got optioned off their teams. I almost quit during the season and then after the season when I went back to Somerset. I told my father, "This is not for me. I'm going with a bunch of optioned players on some shit team."

He talked me out of quitting. He said, "Well, try to hang in there for a couple more months." Things started turning around for me a little bit.

I was way off everybody's radar screen. I didn't know at the end of that season whether I'd be back or not. I had no clue, but I made it through. I started in Stockton, California, and I did not have a good year. I struck out more than 100 times. I couldn't believe I struck out that much. I wasn't a swing-and-miss guy. The only fun part about playing in that league was my roommate, Danny Briggs, and I were also the clubhouse managers. We'd stay after the game and drink a few beers. We'd clean the clubhouse, clean the spikes, get the uniforms washed, and we'd pick up a few extra bucks from the players to do that. I think meal money in those days was like $5 a day or something. We had one trip when we missed the team bus but we had the uniforms. We were going to Bakersfield and we had to jump in Danny's car and drive and we were well behind the time we're supposed to be there. We had all the uniforms in the back of a Volkswagen. We pull into the ballpark in Bakersfield and the manager, Mike Stubbins, was standing out there in his underwear with his arms folded as we pull up in this VW bug. And we just handed out the uniforms and oh, was he pissed. We played that night but it wasn't a good all-around year for me.

The next year they sent me to Davenport, Iowa, which was A-ball. And that's where things started to take off for me. That's the year that I led the league in hitting with a .335 average and I caught the attention of the minor league organization. Davenport was right on the Mississippi. Early in the season the river would flood so the ballpark would get half-flooded in right field. And they used to put a rope up and anything over the rope was a ground-rule double if it landed in the water. If it went over the fence it was a home run. We even had games moved to a high school field because of the flooding. But that's where I ran into Dave Collins, who was my roommate and always remained a good friend of mine, and we played together and made the big leagues together. We had an absolute ball. Collins and I used to get up in the morning and we'd call the ballpark to ask whether the game was going to be rained out. If they weren't going to play, we were going to have a hell of a day.

In addition to leading the league in hitting, my other skills started to develop, too. I became a decent second baseman. I could always run. It finally felt like they thought they had a real prospect. At least a player who could play Triple-A or Double-A. I'm not sure they were even thinking of the big leagues at that time. I was never a real smart base runner as far as being able to pick up stuff from pitchers. I got more experience as I got older, but at that particular time I just relied on flat-out speed. We had a lot of fast guys in the Angels organization. Collins was another guy who could fly. We kind of all gravitated toward that style of play. And I think the more that we did, the more we all learned and actually got better. That helped get me to the big leagues.

My parents and my girlfriend, Phoebe, came to Davenport to watch me play for the first time in the minors. Back then there was no Internet, so other than me telling them how I was doing, there was no easy access to my stats. In those days you had to get *The Sporting News* to see what the players were doing. My grandfather was so tough that every time I'd call him I told him I had a great week. I'd never tell him how bad things might have been. As far as he knew, I hit 1.000 and never made an error. I was more honest with my parents but my calls home were always upbeat and positive about the way things were going no matter how they were going.

The next year they moved me to El Paso, which was Double-A. I had Dave Garcia as a manager there. I was also leading that league in hitting and then about the last six weeks they called me to Triple-A. I didn't have enough at-bats to win the Double-A batting title. But Garcia is the first guy who made me believe that I was going to be a big-leaguer. This all happened pretty quickly, from going to almost released to all of a sudden having Garcia say, "You're going to be a big-leaguer."

I remember him coming up to me one day and saying, "Let me ask you a question. Who runs better, you or Denny Doyle?" Denny was a second baseman for the Angels.

"I do."

"Who's got more range, you or Denny Doyle?"

"I think I do."

"Who hits better, you or Denny Doyle?"

"Well, I led a couple of leagues in hitting. I think I do."

"Well, what makes you think you're not going to be in the big leagues?"

"Well, I don't know."

In those days in Double-A, you couldn't see the big leagues. It's not like today where you have a bunch of guys in spring training camp and where you at least get a taste of what the big leagues are like. We didn't know any of the big-leaguers. It was all minor league. You never smelled anything that had to do with major league baseball. But there was a lot more teaching and time spent learning the game.

Garcia worked me pretty hard. He would take me to the outfield and make me throw long to strengthen my arm to help me on pivots to get a little more on my throws. He was the best. He was a pure backer of mine. Kenny Myers continued to do his thing when he'd come into town. And so, I started to gather some people behind me who were pushing me. I eventually got called up to Triple-A Salt Lake City with about four to six weeks left in the season. Norm Sherry was the manager there. I found Triple-A so different because the attitude was terrible. It was like a collection of the players who had been in big leagues but had been demoted. They were all pissed off because they weren't in the big leagues. It seemed like most of the prospects were in Double-A and then they needed a second baseman, so they called me up. I really wasn't crazy about it. It was like I missed my friends. I missed Dave Collins a lot. And these guys were just playing out the string. I hit a combined .323 between El Paso and Salt Lake City so I proved I could hit. I think I proved to myself that I was ready for the big leagues. I can't say it was a great experience at Triple-A, but it was one I didn't have to experience again because the next year I made the big leagues.

Before that, however, they sent me to winter ball in Mexico, and lucky for me, Garcia managed the Yaquis de Obregon. We were in Ciudad Obregon in Sonora. I remember they were allowed like six American players per team so Dave took me, Jerry Turner—who used to play for the Padres—Don Kirkwood, Dany Briggs, and a couple more guys. But we got off to a horrible start. In winter ball, when you get off to a bad start, they just want to get rid of all the Americans they can and bring in some other guys. But Dave fought for us and we were kind of hoping that he wouldn't because, honestly, none of us liked it. We wanted to go home.

The Mexico experience was like something I'd never seen in my life. The fans bet like crazy on the games in the stands. Sometimes I'd be playing second base and would see the people in the stands just separate, and the next thing you know there were real live snakes flying across the stands. There were beer bottles flying across. This would go on every night. It was dangerous. Then after the games, you'd have to walk through the crowd because there was no clubhouse. You didn't know what was going to happen because they were betting on you and betting against you. Even when I got six hits in a game to tie the record, it was one of those weird days. People were going nuts about it. I said, "What's going on? What are they doing?" I tied some guy named Diablo Montoya. All of a sudden, the fans loved me.

I had one other big reason for not wanting to be there: I had just married my fiancée, Phoebe. We thought it was going to be a three-month honeymoon to Mexico. Well, it wasn't quite like that. It wasn't the honeymoon that we expected. We weren't on the beach. We were living right in the middle of Mexico and it was a culture shock to say the least. Phoebe was sick the whole time down there and I figured if we can make it through this, we can make it through anything. Of course, our team got hot. We ended up in the playoffs!

I had met Phoebe at Empire's Men Shop in Fall River where I sold clothing in the off-season. Phoebe was hired as seasonal help at Christmas, wrapping presents. When we first got married, we lived with her parents in their basement during the off-season. We actually did that until I got traded to the Red Sox in the winter of 1977. During the three years I played with the Angels, we had a place out there that we rented in California. Then we bought a place in Mission Viejo, and of course that year was the year I got traded to the Red Sox.

The Show

When I got to the big leagues, my god, it was amazing. My dad was at my first big-league game with the Angels. I was playing for Dick Williams, who had been the manager of the '67 Red Sox team that we all loved so much. Dad saw my first at-bat, which was a base hit to left field over Kansas City righty Steve Busby on April 7, 1975. I was batting eighth in the lineup that day. And I got a base hit to left field that drove in a run. But on the very next play Busby pulled the old fake to third and throw to first, and he picked me off first.

I knew I screwed up. My first at-bat, I get a hit and get picked off! And I knew I really screwed up when Williams called me over as soon as I got in the dugout. My legs were still shaking from getting a hit. He made me sit right down next to him and he said, "If that fucking happens one more time, your ass is going to be back in Salt Lake City quicker than you can snap your fingers." And I'll never forget it because it was Dick Williams. But I never told my father that.

Grover Resinger, who was Dick Williams' right-hand man, came to Triple-A when I was there. He was another crusty old baseball guy. He was a third-base coach for the White Sox for many years. He came up to me one day and he said he was watching me play and he'd seen me in uniform. He told me he thought I was going to be in the big leagues next year. I said to myself, "Who is this guy?" I'd never met him in my life. So, I went up to Norm Sherry and I said, "Who's the old guy over here? The bald-headed guy. He just told me I'm going to be in the big leagues next year."

He said, "Oh, that's Dick Williams' lieutenant."

I said, "Wow!" I took his word for it, but I truly expected to go back to Triple-A and play a full season. I didn't expect to go to the big leagues.

But when I got to spring training camp, I was in a lucky position because they were going with youth. Denny Doyle was the second baseman. A real class act, too. He knew he was on his way out. That year he went to Boston and they went to the World Series. Later, I replaced him in Boston, too. When I got to spring training, they kept playing me with the shortstop I'd been with in Single-A and Double-A, Orlando Ramirez. They'd always put us in as a combination. And I remember with about probably a week and a half left in spring training, Dick called me in and told me I'd made the team. I couldn't believe it.

I remember asking Grover, "How did this happen so quickly?"

He said, "Williams looked into your eyes and he saw no fear."

And I said, "Okay, but there's got to be more to it."

15

Grover said, "You can play a little bit, too."

I was 22 and the first calls I made were to Phoebe and then my parents. There was definitely some disbelief. They had known that the last few years in the minor leagues had gone pretty well. They knew there was a chance I'd make it to the majors. But that step to the next level…all of a sudden you're in camp and you see Nolan Ryan throwing on the side. And I looked and I said, "Oh, man. If everybody throws like this, I got no chance."

And then I saw Frank Tanana, and man, could he throw back then. We had great pitching, but we had no offense at all. Mickey Rivers was on that team. I think Dave Collins made that team, too.

Bobby Bonds, Don Baylor, and me in the Angels dugout. I got traded to my hometown Red Sox in late 1977. (Getty Images)

But we just had guys who could run. That's the same year that Bill Lee said that if we took batting practice in a hotel lobby we wouldn't break any lights or something like that. Then he went out and stuck it to us that day. Dick Williams was so pissed because Dick loved to go in and play the Red Sox. He just wanted to beat them so bad.

My first major league salary was $16,500. Phoebe and I bought a big station wagon and we drove cross-country from Anaheim to Boston and back. But then we still lived with my wife's parents down in their basement in the off-season. Harry Dalton, who was the Angels' general manager, gave me a bonus of $500 a month during the off-season after my rookie season because I made the All-Rookie team. In my second year, I went up to $22,500. It doesn't sound like much, but it was big-league money and I knew if I kept improving I'd have a chance to make a nice living at it.

I hired Jerry Kapstein as my agent after my second year. Jerry was the best agent in baseball at the time. He had so many big names and he was the agent everyone wanted to have negotiate for them. He remained a lifelong friend, and later helped me land the broadcasting job. I met him in Baltimore. He represented Andy Etchebarren. Jerry was standing in the dugout one day before a game and introduced himself and said he was from Rhode Island. And I had heard of him, obviously, so I was ecstatic that he wanted me as a client. He had friggin' 80 percent of baseball at that time.

I loved the fact that we were building something with the Angels and a lot of guys I came up with were on the major league team with me. Dick Williams was fired during my second year and Sherry took over, which was fine since I had played for Norm at Triple-A Salt Lake City. Norm kind of shocked the world out there when he named me the captain during the 1976 season. I was pretty shocked, too. Norm was looking for a young leader to reflect the team and he thought I had leadership skills and he respected the way I played the game. People questioned why he would name a 24-year-old player with 2½ years' experience the captain, but he had his reasons. He told Ross Newhan, who was the top baseball writer out in Los Angeles at the time, "We've been so up and down that maybe Jerry can help stabilize it. I know he's young, but he plays hard and he had his teammates' respect in that he's not afraid to speak out, to assert himself. I told him to be himself and say whatever he feels he needs to say."

I think at the time we were starting to turn the corner. I thought our attitude was improving as a team. The year before, I had won the Owner's Trophy as the team's most valuable player. So, I guess I had asserted myself in a positive way. Of course, Norm was fired and replaced with Garcia not long afterward. We finished 74–88, fifth in the AL West. My captaincy was short-lived. It was my last season with the Angels as well.

Traded to My Hometown

The winter meetings were in Hawaii in December of 1977. My agent, Jerry Kapstein, was one of the most influential people in baseball and he knew how much I wanted to come home and play for the Red Sox. I really believe that he was the guy who got me to Boston. The Angels were talking about two places, San Diego and Boston. I told Jerry, "I've got to get home." I had already played three years on the West Coast. It was great because it was my introduction to the big leagues. I was playing with all the kids I'd played with in the minor leagues. And my wife loved it out there. I don't know how much Jerry had to do with it, but there was a lot of tugging and pulling to get me to Boston, I think.

When I got that phone call, I couldn't believe it. My wife was not happy, but I was ecstatic to play alongside Yaz and Dwight Evans and Jim Rice, Carlton Fisk, Fred Lynn, Butch Hobson, and Rick Burleson. I was going back home. I was going to play at Fenway Park.

The first call I got was from Fisk, who called me from New Hampshire and welcomed me to the team. Really nice thing for him to do. He was also a Jerry client. And I heard from Don Zimmer and Haywood Sullivan, who called from Hawaii and said they'd completed the trade and welcome to the Red Sox and all that. And I was out of my mind.

My whole family was really excited. Whenever the Angels were in town to play at Fenway, all the guys would come up. They'd get a little rambunctious and were escorted out of the stadium. My wife was a little apprehensive about how this Boston gig would turn out. It ended up being the best thing that could've happened. It set up our future.

The Red Sox traded a pretty good reliever/spot starter in Don Aase. I'm always asked why the Angels traded me. I was only 25 and was in the prime of my career. What seemed to happen was they loaded up in 1977. They signed Bobby Grich, Joe Rudi, and Don Baylor, three big names. They had moved Bobby to shortstop, but he was hurt a lot in '77. They were able to move Bobby back to second after I was traded.

So that's how the Red Sox thing started. But to get a call from Carlton Fisk? It was like, Jesus. I'm really here. This is unbelievable. And that's just after watching them in the '75 World Series. My goodness.

As excited as I was, it was also tough to leave the Angels because that was really my home. They're the guys who gave me a chance. They're the guys who groomed me. They're the guys who almost released me. They're the guys who took me to the big leagues, and I had all my friends there. We all came up together in the minor leagues. That part was tough, but the easy part was forgetting about that because I was going to Boston. Had I gone to San Diego, it would have been a whole different story. I would not have been happy. Even though I lived out there I was never into the lifestyle the way my wife was. We lived in Mission Viejo and we were 15 minutes from Laguna Beach. She loves the beach and she was there all the time. I was an East Coast guy and I was trying so hard to fit in. I always felt like I had to prove myself every day. For me it was totally about baseball. We never even spent an off-season out there. We'd always come back home. The one year we were going to spend time out there is the year we were traded. We had just bought the condo and we were going to go back after Christmas and spend January and February there, and then go to spring training.

We started our spring training workouts in Holtville and then when we started games we would go to Palm Springs, then fly to Arizona and play a week in Arizona. Palm Springs was so beautiful that nobody even wanted to leave there to go to Anaheim. They'd rather play the season in Palm Springs. It was gorgeous and the weather was great. What also was neat about the Angels was the owner, Gene Autry. He was a great owner. He took care of the players. He loved baseball. He was there almost every game. The only thing about Gene was that he liked his cocktails. And he had Pat Buttram, his sidekick. They would bring him down after a game and he'd be toasted, and they'd be holding him by his arms. He'd have his cowboy boots on and he'd be walking through the clubhouse. I think the only player he really knew was Nolan Ryan. And for some of us he had to look up at the name on the locker and say, "Hi, Jerry. How are you doing?" But he was a good guy. And he was a good fan. He was there a lot.

Mr. Autry had a special day for us every year when he'd take us out to a golf course and ranch that he owned, and we had a family day. We had a wonderful time and he was so generous as an owner.

People always asked me whether he had a lot of celebrities at the games and the answer was no. Even though Mr. Autry was in that business, all of the actors visited up the road with the Dodgers. By the way, we despised the Dodgers. They looked at us as a Triple-A franchise. All the celebs were watching the Dodgers, who were very good at that time. They had the celebrity manager in Tommy Lasorda. We always felt like second-class citizens. They'd fill that place and we'd have 7,000 or 8,000 people at our games, unless Nolan Ryan was pitching or the Red Sox, Yankees, or Tigers came to town.

I speak a lot about my Red Sox teammates, but the Angels teammate I respected most was Ryan. He was the classiest act I've ever been around. When you were a kid back in those days coming to the big leagues, you were treated like shit by a lot of the veteran players. Not him. He was a standup guy, one of the greatest guys I've ever known in the game. He kind of took me under his wing a little bit. I knew I had a veteran superstar player who backed me and who liked me. I found throughout my career that the guys who treated you like shit were guys who were insecure about their jobs. You don't see that in today's game as much. Hardly at all, really. Nolan was top shelf. I mean, to this day, we still get a Christmas card from him. His wife, Ruth, is also terrific.

The other extraordinary pitcher on those Angels teams was Frank Tanana. Back then he could really bring it. He wasn't the finesse pitcher that people remember him as toward the end of his career, after he hurt his arm. Back then Frank was a little young and immature and some people wanted to paint him as another Bo Belinsky, a guy about town, but he was really good. He threw hard, he had a great curve ball. I mean, you threw Ryan out there one day and Tanana the next day, there weren't many hits. Then he hurt his arm and he became a totally different pitcher. He continued to pitch but not like the young Frank Tanana that I saw.

He was awesome. One game sticks out in my mind. We were playing the Oakland A's, who had a great team. They loaded the bases and he struck out three guys in a row. I can't remember exactly who they were, but they were right in the middle of the lineup and he punched them out to get out of the inning. It'd be interesting to see what kind of career he would have had had he not hurt his arm.

In any case, my time in California had come to an end. That chapter in my life was over. I was coming home.

CHAPTER 2
1978

In Boston we know the story all too well. We had a nine-game lead over the Yankees on August 13 and we couldn't hold it. We were forced into a one-game playoff, and we lost it. It was the most disappointing year of my career because we had a great team. But I'll never accept this narrative that we choked. We didn't choke. We were up against a great Yankees team. We fought back to finish strong, but we lost a one-game playoff in the 163rd game of the year.

It was also the most significant year of my career because I'd been traded to my hometown team from the Angels at the winter meetings in 1977. I was not only coming home, I was joining a team with future Hall of Famers like Yaz, Pudge, Jimmy, and Eck, plus a guy who should be in the Hall of Fame, Luis Tiant, and another who could have been a Hall of Famer had he stayed in Boston, Fred Lynn. We also had Dwight Evans, who won eight Gold Gloves and was another guy who should have been considered more seriously for the Hall.

The Red Sox brought me in because they needed a leadoff hitter and a guy who could steal bases at the top of the order. They needed speed. And I had that. That off-season, they also brought in Mike Torrez, who had pitched for the Yankees and wound up starting the playoff game against his old team. We bolstered our bullpen with Dick Drago. In spring training, we made a blockbuster deal that in my opinion got us over the top. We acquired Dennis Eckersley from the Indians and Eck won 20 games for us. On paper we had the best team in baseball. We won 99 games, same as the Yankees, unfortunately.

We knew the Yankees had a great team. We knew how much we hated them. That was ingrained in me as soon as I got to the Red Sox. This was real hatred. They were the enemy. They were the bad guys and we were the good guys. You'll never see this scenario play out again in sports. Nowadays everybody is friendly. Oh, there's competition on the field, but everybody knows the guys on the other team. They may share an agent or have played together in the minors. Back then there were definite lines drawn and I think it was much more fun that way because you had a chip on your shoulder every time you played.

Our Opening Day lineup was kickass. I led off, with Rick Burleson, the most intense player on the team, batting second and playing shortstop. We had Rice hitting third and Yaz cleanup. We had Fisk batting fifth, Lynn sixth, George Scott seventh, Evans eighth, and Butch Hobson ninth. Try to navigate that lineup! Most of the time the other team couldn't. If we hadn't suffered so many injuries the second half of the year, I wonder how many games we would have won. The 2018 team won 108 games. I wonder if we could have matched that or surpassed it. That's how good we were. We also had a very good rotation with Luis Tiant, Torrez, Eckersley, and Bill Lee. We had a great bullpen with Bob Stanley, one of the most underrated pitchers in Red Sox history. He went 15–2 that year with 10 saves. We had Bill "Soup" Campbell and Tom Burgmeier, a tough lefty. Drago played a big role.

We got out to a 51–21 start and to everyone we looked unstoppable. By July 19 we had a nine-game lead over Milwaukee, 12½ games over the Orioles, and 14 over the Yanks. We had won 34 out of our first 40 games at Fenway.

In New York the Yankees were going through their usual soap opera with George Steinbrenner. At one point he suspended Reggie Jackson because Reggie tried to bunt the runners along rather than swing away. There were two strikes and he whiffed for strike three and Billy Martin went into a rage. Steinbrenner called it "on-field disobedience" in justifying the suspension. Steinbrenner fired Martin after they fell 14 games behind us and he hired Bob Lemon, who was a mellow guy, and the Yankees responded by winning 30 of their next 43 games. Our lead over them had gone from 14 to four.

It was a weird time. We knew the lead had slipped away, but even with our injuries, we felt we had the better team and we would prevail. But then, I must admit, the Yankees just punched us in the nose in a series at Fenway that became known as the "Boston Massacre" in early September.

The scores were 15–3, 13–2, 7–0, and 7–4. We were outscored 42–9. We committed 12 errors. We sucked. We deserved every bit of criticism that came our way.

Our manager, Don Zimmer, decided he was going to give rookie Bobby Sprowl a start over Bill Lee. Zin really disliked Lee, but Lee was the obvious choice because he was pitching really well in long relief. Zim didn't see it the way 99 percent of Red Sox Nation saw it. Sprowl had pitched one major league game. He had allowed three runs over seven innings in his only start. He seemed like a tough kid who could handle the moment. At least Zim thought so.

Unfortunately, Sprowl gave up three runs in the first inning. Not a great start for our team. Zim yanked him before he could get through the first and brought in Bob Stanley, our jack of all trades. "Steamer" had been a great pitcher for us. He's one of the greatest Red Sox relievers of all time. He threw that heavy sinker, got ground balls. But on this day, he got hit around by a relentless Yankees lineup, allowing 10 hits over three innings. We got three runs off Ed Figueroa over six innings, but we knew the Yankees had Goose Gossage waiting in the bullpen.

We lost a couple of more games in New York a few days later and now all of a sudden, we were 3½ games behind the Yankees. We were stunned. It felt like we were getting pummeled in a heavyweight fight and we were staggering. We did win the last game of that Yankees series and started to feel like we could recover. We won 11 out of our last 13 and we forced a tie with the Yankees. We won the coin flip to gain the home-field advantage for the game. At least we beat them on that.

I remember being at home the night before. We're packing our suitcases, because whoever wins that game goes on to Kansas City. We were totally expecting to win. The game itself was a great game. It was one of the best games in history. It was a clean game. It was well played by both teams. Well-pitched, clutch hitting, great defense.

I had never been so nervous in my life playing a game—or starting a game, I should say—than I was in that one. We felt confident in Mike Torrez. We wished Eckersley was available, but he wasn't.

The good thing was that we were home. The bad thing was we were going up against Ron Guidry, who was the best pitcher in baseball in 1978. He was 25–3. His "Louisiana Lightning" nickname was fitting. The guy was untouchable all season. He struck out 248 batters. I still remember feeling confident we could win the game. We had to use Luis Tiant to win that 162nd game so we entered the game with Torrez, who had a very good year for us. We thought Torrez had big-time incentive to beat his old team.

And for most of this game, I was right. Yaz belted a solo homer and that made us feel more comfortable. Jimmy knocked in a second run. We had a 2–0 lead over Guidry who wasn't himself, throwing more sliders than fastballs in the first six innings. Both Guidry and Torrez were pitching on just three days' rest. They were both running on fumes. In the seventh, Chris Chambliss and Roy White reached on singles, with Bucky Dent coming up. Dent hit a high fly ball to left. It would have been an out in virtually every other major league stadium. But at Fenway, it found a way to clear the Green Monster. We were stunned. Shocked. Choose an adjective. It was 3–2, Yankees.

Bucky Dent's home run to beat us in the one-game playoff against the Yankees in 1978. (AP Images)

And then, well, Guidry was pulled with one out in the seventh and Goose Gossage came in. Gossage was obviously one of the best closers in the game. In the eighth we scored two runs on RBI singles by Yaz and Lynn. I had doubled, one of my two hits in the game.

It was a 5–4 game heading into the ninth. Burleson, who led off in the game because of the lefty Guidry pitching, walked, and I then singled. It wasn't just any single. I hit a line drive toward

Lou Piniella in right field. Piniella never saw it. Even our third-base coach Eddie Yost had trouble judging it. He was frantically waving Burleson around to score, but Rick had no idea if Piniella was going to catch it or keep it in front of him or whether it would roll to the wall. As it was, Piniella kept it in front of him. "I went to where I thought it would land," Piniella told the media after the game. "I saw it when it hit and reacted." Burleson stayed at second base. If he had made it to third he would have scored on Rice's fly ball. Instead he was on third with two outs.

It was one of those topspin line drives and I don't think Piniella would have caught it anyway. I don't think he would have taken a chance at coming in and having that ball get by him and have a run score from first base. But then, I didn't realize until I was about halfway down the line that he had lost the ball in the sun. Then, he just reaches out with his glove to his left, and the ball pops right into his glove. He didn't even know it. If the ball got by him, Burleson would have scored and I'd be at third base.

I'd have had a statue out at Fenway if that ball had dropped in and got by Piniella because there was an outside chance I could have had an inside-the-park home run, and we would have won.

And then Yaz came up with two on and two outs. Gossage vs. Yaz. What a way to end it. It was fastball pitcher vs. fastball hitter. Gossage had some amazing things to say after the game.

"I wasn't going to mess around with breaking junk and get beaten by anything but my best," said Gossage. "Yastrzemski's the greatest player I've ever played against. I just wound up and threw it as hard as I could. I couldn't tell you where."

Yaz thought the 1-0 pitch was going to tail to the outside, but it came in. He tried to hold up but he swung through and the ball popped up high into foul territory off third base. Yaz knew he missed it. Graig Nettles secured the ball. It was over.

I'll never forget that after Nettles caught the ball, as I was heading back toward the Red Sox dugout, how completely silent the crowd was except for the Yankees fans there. But everyone was stunned. I could see faces that were just in disbelief that this game was over, and that we had lost. The worst feeling in the world was driving home that night with this suitcase that you had packed to go to Kansas City, and having to watch the Yankees play the Royals the following day.

It was the first time I'd ever seen Yaz cry. He took that loss so hard. He knew he had a chance to win the game and he couldn't do it. He was heartbroken. We were so close. It was just a devastating loss. We had everything set up for a dramatic walkoff win. Instead we walked off the losers. And what has always bothered me is that team never received its just due.

It was a pretty eerie feeling in the clubhouse after the game. We were called bums after that. It was like we were chokers, we were this, we were that. I couldn't believe it, because we won 99 games, and went to a playoff game, and lost by one run, and we're chokers because we gave up the big lead. I'm going, my god, if that team's not good enough to be called a good team, what is?

The Names and Faces of '78

When I got traded to Boston I got a call from Fisk, who had grown up in Vermont and was living in New Hampshire. He welcomed me and that was quite a thrill for me, because here's another local kid. Of course, we all knew all about his 1975 heroics, and the waving of the ball fair in Game 6 of the World Series.

You couldn't help obsessing over that '78 season. It was the tale of two seasons, really. The first half belonged to the Red Sox, and the second half belonged to the Yankees. When you evened it all out, it came down to a dead tie. Playing on that team in the first half of the season, we had the feeling we just couldn't be beat. Nobody could beat us at Fenway Park. It was that kind of an offense that we knew we'd always strike back, no matter what the score was. We just had total confidence we were going to win those games. We built up an incredible lead by the All-Star break, which fell apart in the second half for a lot of reasons.

Number one, the Yankees played as well in the second half as we had in the first half. We didn't play very good baseball, and we had a bunch of injuries. Not to make excuses, but the fact is we had Fisk playing with a broken rib, and Hobson had chips moving in his elbow every time he threw a ball. Burleson went out for a while with an eye problem. We had our issues. I went down on August 25 with a chipped bone in my left wrist after Angels outfielder Rick Miller slid into me stealing second in the first inning. Dwight Evans got dizzy when he ran as a result of an August 28 beaning and hit .161 (9-for-56) in September with one home run and three RBIs.

When all was said and done, I felt all year that the Yankees and the Red Sox were the two best teams in baseball, and I think all of us, probably on both teams, felt that way. We thought one of us was going win the World Series. That's exactly what happened and the Yankees went on to beat the Dodgers.

Burleson, our shortstop, was one of the most intense guys I ever played with in my life. We kind of hit it off because our personalities were very similar. We got together early in spring training and we were hard to separate, because we were trying to learn each other as a second baseman and shortstop, and also as people. We found out we had an awful lot in common. Nobody got pissed off quicker than "Rooster" did. I might have been second in that category, but he brought an intensity around the bag that I had never experienced before in the big leagues. He had a fabulous arm. I hated to play catch with him, because from his first throw, he'd be throwing as hard as he possibly could. He was amazing. He wouldn't warm up. He'd just start firing. Just playing catch with him, prior to a game, was a challenge, because everything was a bullet. That's how he played shortstop. Nothing was easy. Everything was balls-out all the time.

He had good range, too. He was also very good at making the pivot at second base. One of the funny stories about him that year is we had a big series coming up with the Yankees at Fenway Park. Rooster had popped off in the press about the Yankees. The next day, the headline was about how Burleson hates all the Yankees. It was like, "Oh my god, what is this all about?" The Yankees didn't appreciate that very much, and they were coming in at second base trying to kill us that whole series because of the comments that he made.

The aftermath of '78 was sad for me. Tiant went over to the Yankees. In spring training of 1979, I remember Zimmer telling us, "Any time you get on first base today, let's run on Luis." Thurman Munson was catching, and we didn't realize he had a sore arm.

When we started the official season, he says, "Did you guys have fun with me in spring training?" We didn't know what the hell he was talking about.

I said, "No, Zim told us just have a little fun with Luis."

He says, "You didn't realize that I had a bad arm?"

What I wanted to say was, "If you had a bad arm, you shouldn't have been catching in that game." But I didn't say it, so he was pissed and that's something he never forgot. It was that kind of a chippy relationship between everybody.

Then, we had Hobson at third base, who was this tough Alabama kid. Just a guy who lived hard and played hard. I wouldn't call him the most talented third baseman in baseball. He made a bunch of errors, but he had power. He was a guy at the bottom of the lineup who could hit home runs for us and drive in runs. He was playing hurt all year. He had these bone chips in his elbow and it was painful to watch him throw the ball. Instead of having surgery, he'd just keep moving around the chips into a place where he could throw comfortably. He was doing that just about all year. But he was another guy that was in the Burleson mode of going balls-out all the time. He was a football player at Alabama, played for Bear Bryant. He had that kind of mentality and he was very tough.

We had Jimmy Rice, who had the best year I've ever seen anybody have. I mean, he did everything that year for us. He hit home runs. I think he led the league in total bases. He was just the guy you wanted at the plate in key situations. People always talk about his power, but he also had a very good batting average. You think of the two monster home runs he hit in the game, but then, you'd look in the paper, and he also had four hits, and you'd go, "Where did the other hits go?" You didn't remember those, but you remember the monster home runs that he would hit, and he also played a damn good left field. He played that wall very well. That's something he got better and better at, as time went on, and by the time I got there, he was really good at playing that wall.

The other thing about Jimmy is he never took a day off. I mean, I remember him going to the dentist and getting wisdom teeth pulled and playing that night, where other guys would be out for a couple of days. He was also very quiet, and he wasn't fond of the media. He just wanted to play baseball and be left alone. He had some issues with members of the media. He threw Thomas Boswell from *The Washington Post* into a rubbish barrel. He picked him up and threw him right in the trash can. He was so strong.

In my stretch with the Red Sox, he's probably the best player that I played with because he was in the prime of his career, and he was there longer than the other guys. The other guys either left because of free agency or got traded. You just had the feeling that every time Jimmy came to the plate, he was going to do something big, and in '78, he did. He did everything big.

We hit it off, and while I wouldn't say we were close, I was probably as close as anyone was going to get to Jimmy. I always felt like he was a guy who I could go up to and have some laughs with, and talk to, whereas I don't think others felt the same way.

As for Fred Lynn, in my mind, had he spent his whole career in Boston, he probably would have been a Hall of Famer. The reason I say that is because Fenway was built for him, and I also think that extra little push that you get from playing in Boston would have pushed him to a higher level than maybe playing somewhere else. He could do everything. He was a great center fielder. He was a great hitter. He could use the wall anytime he wanted to use it. He was a very good base runner. He had a good, strong throwing arm. He was just a totally different personality than the guys I've mentioned so far. He was very laid-back. Very Southern Californian. Not that all guys from Southern California are laid-back, but he was. Not much bothered him. He was kind of just relaxed. He took whatever results came. That was pretty much it.

I wouldn't call the relationship between Jim and Fred close, from what I could tell. When Fred got the Rookie of the Year in 1975 and Jimmy didn't, that may have had something to do with it. I mean, I can't say they were enemies. Over the years, they developed a closer relationship.

Then, you had Dwight Evans. "Dewey," at that stage of his career, was finding himself as a hitter. He was always a great outfielder. Even when I was playing with the Angels, the rumor was you didn't hit it out to right field. If Evans is out there, you don't try to take the extra base. That was the scouting report. I was lucky enough to see that firsthand when I became a member of the Red Sox. He could play right field like nobody's business. He was so quick at getting balls into second base, or making that spin move and throwing somebody out at third base. It was a pleasure to watch. He got hooked up with Walt Hriniak, and I think Walt did wonders for his career, offensively.

Walt wasn't the official hitting coach in 1978, but five or six guys used him as that. Jimmy used Johnny Pesky, but Yaz and Fisk and myself and Dwight all used Walt, who was the best coach that I'd ever had in my life. He had a certain style which gave him a bad rap because hitters looked like clones, but there were others who worked with him who didn't look like that at all. I think that he got a horrible rap here in Boston with the people who worked for the organization, because you had Ted Williams, who would come to spring training where it was his way or the highway.

Nobody could really understand what Walt was teaching us. He was teaching the Charlie Lau method of hitting, which was very popular in those days. Some guys had completely different looking stances than what they did before he got a hold of them. He got the bad reputation of, "Well, he is trying to make everybody the same." That's not true. I wasn't the same as Dwight and Yaz wasn't the same as Dwight. Walt kind of worked with you individually to get the most out of you. He had certain beliefs, but it's not like he demanded we do this or that. I think the combination with him and Evans really clicked. Dwight became a really good hitter under the tutelage of Hriniak.

He also helped me incredibly, because I went from a guy who hit a lot of fly balls that went about 280 feet for outs to more of a line-drive, ground-ball type hitter, which turned me into a .300 hitter. What he did for my career was unbelievable. The other thing about him is he couldn't sleep at night if we didn't hit. He was so involved as a person and a coach that he lived and died with everything we did. He knew when to talk to people and when not to talk to people. For example, if I had a bad game, I didn't want to talk to anybody. He knew that. He'd wait until the next day, and when I'd get there early, then we'd have a chat about the night before, and what's going on, and go back out and work on it. He was an amazing man. He broke his right arm doing flips one day, and he tried to learn how to throw left-handed so he could still throw batting practice. That's how crazy he was.

We had George Scott at first base, the best defensive first baseman I ever played with. You had total confidence that every throw over there, "Boomer" was going to catch. On balls that were hit between first and second base, he'd love to show off his range, going toward the second base bag. He loved making that backhanded play and then throwing to the pitcher covering. What I thought was funny was after a while, he said to me, "Call me off that ball. Call me off that ball." He really didn't want to be called off the ball because he wanted to make the play, so I'd just say, "Yeah, Boomer, okay. No problem. I'll call you off." He just kept doing the same thing over and over, even if I called him off.

He had just a smooth glove, and, boy, did he save errors. Even off-balance throws from second on double plays, we didn't worry about it because we knew that he was going to pick it at the other end. I think his best hitting days were behind him by then, but he never lost it with the glove. He could still put a hurting on you with some home runs and stuff like that at that time, but I don't think he was as offensively effective, in that particular time, as he was earlier in his career.

Then, you had Fisk behind the plate. There was always this raging debate between who was the best, Fisk or Munson. There was also another guy who was very good down in Texas, Jim Sundberg, a very good defensive catcher. I'm partial to Fisk, because I played with him. He was a giant behind the plate. He was so big. You don't see a lot of really tall catchers. He had the ability to be very flexible and get down as low as he possibly could to give pitchers good targets.

He had a great throwing arm. He threw directly over the top. He threw cross-seamed fastballs to second base, where Munson would throw kind of almost like three-quarters. Munson was so quick that if he made a good throw, he'd get you by five feet, but a lot of his throws would end up going into center field, because he'd bounce them. It was really a gamble running on him. You either were going to be safe by quite a distance, or you were going to be out by five feet. You never knew which throw was going to be a good one for him. Fisk was another disciple of Hriniak. He was just a clutch hitter. He was a great base runner for a big guy. I think he might have been our best base runner.

Behind the plate, he was definitely in charge. There was no question about that. I think the pitchers probably got sick of him going to the mound, but if he had something to say, he'd be out there. There was that famous picture of him taking the mask and putting it on top of his head, walking out to the mound. In those days, he was slow and methodical, but if he had something to say, he'd say it to you. There was no bullshitting around with him. He was to the point, not with just pitchers but with everybody. He was pretty incredible. Again, the best catcher I had ever been around.

Our manager was Don Zimmer. Zim was totally different than anybody else I'd played for. I played for Dick Williams. I played for Norm Sherry. I played for Dave Garcia with the Angels. And then all of a sudden, I've got Zim, who was totally a position player's manager. He didn't care for pitchers. I don't know where that came from. A lot of people think it came from when he was beaned, when he was younger. He pretty much ran the same lineup out there every day. He was one of those guys who didn't do a lot of platooning.

A couple of funny stories about Zim. There was one time I was struggling against left-handers, in '78 or '79. Zim sat me down against a couple left-handers in a row. I went to Hriniak and I said, "Walt, what is going on here? Why am I not playing against these left-handers?" I realized I wasn't hitting them that good but Zim never changed the lineup. Walt told me to go in and ask Zim. I made the mistake of doing just that. Zim must have been waiting on me, because I knocked on the door and before it even got out of my mouth, he was chewing my ass out about even having the balls to come in and ask him why I wasn't playing. He started rattling off these numbers. He was screaming so I walked out. I went up to Hriniak and I said, "Thanks for having me go in there. Christ. I just got my ass chewed out for 10 minutes."

The other funny story was we were playing at Fenway one day, and I attempted to steal second base and got thrown out. Zim called me in and he asks, "Did you check the way the wind was blowing?" I said, "What are you talking about?" He said, "Well, the wind's blowing straight out. When you've got guys like Yastrzemski and Rice and Fisk hitting behind you, you don't get thrown out at second base with the wind blowing out at Fenway Park."

That became a little bit difficult for me, because I was there for speed. I think I stole 30 in '78, and 22 of those came on the road, because Zim didn't want me running at Fenway. I don't think those guys hitting behind me were crazy about me running, anyway. That was especially true for Yaz, because if he had a hole at first base, he wanted that hole there. He didn't want you running to take away the hole. When I was on second base, I was already in scoring position. He didn't even want you moving at second base, because it would distract him. It was kind of a touchy situation because I came from a team where all we did was run.

Yaz was real quiet. He pretty much kept to himself. Off the field, he and Dewey would go out to dinner a lot together. But he was really focused on what he had to do. He DH'd a lot and was playing first base by the time I got to Boston, but he still played some left field and still played it great. He had no fear of the wall at all. He'd go crashing into it and try to make plays, and he became a pretty decent first baseman too, when they moved him over there.

We had an underrated pitching staff. Campbell had a very good year out of the bullpen. Stanley was incredibly valuable to us. He

Jim Rice and I meeting the great Carl Yastrzemski at the plate in 1978. (AP Images)

filled every role that was possible. He'd start games if he had to. He'd come in and throw five innings in the middle of the game. He worked toward the end of the game. He'd be a setup guy. He'd close if he had to. He had a rubber arm.

Eck really was the key to our '78 season. I remember playing against him. He no-hit us when I was with the Angels. He didn't even realize he was doing it, but what he was doing was after he'd strike somebody out, or they'd get an out, he'd point to the guy in the batter's box to get in the box next. You can't imagine how bad you wanted to get a hit off him. None of us wanted the game to end, because we wanted to break up that no-hitter. He was kind of the same way with the Sox. He just wore his emotions on his sleeve. When he was good, he was really good. He would piss the opponents off with his antics on the mound. But it didn't matter at that time, because he was so good.

And there was Bill Lee. I can't say I knew him very well. I'm not sure anybody did, except maybe Jim Willoughby and Bernie Carbo. He was in his own world. But one of the biggest disappointments of the year, for me, was when we were playing a big series against the Yankees, and Zimmer decided to pitch Bobby Sprowl instead of Lee. Zimmer disliked Lee. He couldn't stand him. I don't know if that came into his thinking of who he started, but it really hurt us in that game. Sprowl was awful and Lee was going to put at least a competitive performance out there for you. But the one thing I remember about Lee is he'd take a lot of pressure off you, because he would go off on these rants with the media, and kind of draw attention away from what might be going on with us. The reporters would flock to his locker because they never knew what the hell he was going to say. He once called Zim a gerbil. You have to understand how that went over.

Then you had Tiant, who was the complete opposite, just the ultimate professional. He'd go out there every game expecting to pitch nine innings. The tougher the competition, the better for him. A great, great, great teammate. One of the funniest guys I've ever met in my life. Some of the conversations between him and Yaz were just absolutely hilarious, and Boomer, too. They were just absolutely hilarious to listen to. Tiant would constantly be on George Scott. Constantly. Then, he'd be all over Yaz, too, about his clothes.

Yaz was really cheap. He never went out and bought shit. One day Dick Drago threw a leather jacket in the trash at Fenway, in the clubhouse. Yaz saw him. He went into the trash, took it out, and asked, "What are you throwing this away for?" Drago said, "Well, it's all worn out and stuff." Yaz took it out of the barrel, slapped some things on the elbows, some suede pads or something, and wore it the rest of the year.

Of course, Tiant would see something like that and just completely tear into him. But Luis was great, because if you made a mistake behind Luis, he'd call you to the mound and say, "Don't worry about it. You get the next one." You always had a comfort level playing behind him. You weren't afraid to make mistakes, because he was the kind of guy who would not let that bother him. He knew he wasn't perfect, and he knew nobody else was perfect.

It was a pleasure to play behind him. He was so damn competitive. He was so funny. I remember somebody hit a home run against him in '78. When contact was made, I heard Luis going, "Oh, my god" on the mound. This was a real bomb. It wasn't coming back. He could do stuff like that. And you could hear jingling all the time. I don't know if it was change, or I don't know if he had his wallet in his pocket. I don't know what it was. He was the guy who really loosened everybody up in the clubhouse.

* * *

It was a tough off-season. We felt we had another good team in '79, even though we lost Luis to the Yankees. We felt like we were going to have a run of about three to four years that were going to be special. As a team we felt we were going to win it. But I screwed up my knee in '79, sliding into home plate at Yankee Stadium. It was a terrible play on my part. There was a little fly ball down the first-base line. I thought Chris Chambliss was going to catch it. But Willie Randolph caught it instead and I tagged up and tried to score on it. I was out by probably seven feet. I tried to slide around the tag and I got my spike caught. That's when I first tore my knee up. I didn't get to play a lot the rest of that year. I played in 80 games total. Fisk played in just 91 games.

We wound up winning 91 games, but that was only good enough for third. We were 11½ games behind the Orioles. There were some good individual years. Lynn led the league with a .333 average and had 39 homers and 122 RBIs. Rice batted .325, with 39 homers and 130 RBIs. Eck won 17 and Torrez had 16 wins.

Yaz got his 3,000th hit and hit his 400th home run. His 3,000th hit came against Jim Beattie on September 12. It was a single.

I don't think there was a hangover effect but there was a lot of pressure on us after we took it to the limit the year before. We were called failures for not getting it done, and we felt like we had something to prove to everybody. It's hard to prove when you have already won 99. It's really hard to feel like, okay, we have to win 105. I mean, those things don't generally happen.

CHAPTER 3
MY COACHING CAREER

My coaching career didn't last very long, but I enjoyed it and I had some good kids to teach. I only coached the home games, so I never had to ride the buses like a lot of minor league coaches and managers do.

It was 1986 and the Red Sox had started to have a pretty good crop of talent. I had future major-leaguers like Ellis Burks, Jody Reed, Sam Horn, Jim Corsi, and John Marzano on the Double-A New Britain Red Sox. We played at a very large old ballpark called Beehive Field. It was definitely more of a pitcher's park. The Double-A Red Sox played there from 1983 to 1994.

Burks was terrific at the minor league level. You could talk to him about something and he'd go out and do it. Ellis was just a great kid. He is a great example for everybody else. He was a high draft choice and a guy we knew was going to be a big-leaguer, and he knew he was probably going to be a star in the big leagues, but you'd never know it by his actions. He was so approachable and such a good guy that everything that he got, he deserved. He had a great career. He had trouble in Boston with his back but then he got healthy and he put up big numbers in Chicago, Colorado, and San Francisco. Ellis wound up with 352 home runs and hit .291 for his career. It was great that he was able to end his career with the Red Sox in 2004. While Ellis got hurt and wasn't able to play much, I know he had a big role on the bench and in the clubhouse as a positive influence. Yeah, he was special, and you could see that at Double-A. He was a guy that stood out at every game.

The one funny story I have about that year was dealing with Marzano, who unfortunately died very young at the age of 45. He was a first-round pick, 14th overall in the 1984 draft, but his style was one that I didn't particularly warm up to.

One night I was coaching first base and he hit a ground ball to shortstop. Like most other grounders he hit, he didn't run it out.

This would really irritate me because I drilled home to all of my players to run hard down the line, because running hard is one thing you can control.

I always kept a stopwatch with me at first base and I would time guys down the line. One night, we're playing a game and he's the last hitter of the game, and he grounded out. He never ran hard to first base. He just jogged down there and never touched first base and the game was over.

So I kept the clock going and I never shut it off. I put it in my locker overnight and I let it run the whole next day until Marzano came to the ballpark. I told him, "John, come here. Do you want to see your time to first base last night?" I showed him the clock, and I think he got the message about running down the line.

It was one of those kinds of things that I enjoyed doing as a coach. I wanted to teach the kids to play the game the right way. And when I did something that got my point across, I felt I had succeeded as a coach.

It's funny because I enjoyed coaching the guys you knew weren't going to make it as much as I did the ones who did make it. Those first guys busted their asses down the line. They were out on the field early every day trying to get better. They didn't take anything for granted. They would go through a wall to try to impress you. But most of them never made it. And that's sad for me because those kids had dreams, and as hard as they tried they were never going to take that leap to the big leagues (even though they deserved a lot of credit for getting as high as Double-A, which isn't easy to do).

Quite frankly, it was tough on me. I wanted these kids to succeed. That was the most difficult part of coaching because you worked just as hard with those kids as you did with the high draft picks who were going to make it and you just wished there was something you could do to get them over the hump. But as a big-leaguer myself I knew that most of them didn't have the skill set to make it.

I remember that Reed was really struggling at Double-A, and he was a guy who was going to play in the big leagues. That was plain to see. He was hitting about .228 and I had a beef with Lou Gorman because Lou called me to get my opinion about calling him up to Triple-A. They needed somebody at Triple-A but I was against it. I wanted him to fight out of this slump. I thought it was important to do that because when you're in the big leagues and you're in a slump, you've got to fight out of it. There's no place to hide, and I felt like it would be more beneficial for him to remain at Double-A after being in this terrible slide and fight his way out of it and end up having a decent year. And I thought that would serve him well throughout his career.

I told Lou how I felt, but they would have none of it. They wanted him to go up. And he went to Triple-A and he had a fresh start. That .229 average that he was carrying at Double-A was gone, and I guess he had a pretty decent year at Triple-A, hitting .282. Eventually I guess I was wrong, but that's how I thought at the time. I thought, let's teach this kid at this particular level how to fight out of a slump, how to battle through a year, how to fight through adversity. I thought that would be more important for him in the long run than giving him a fresh start.

That's also the same year that I had Glenn Hoffman, who had been the major league shortstop with the Red Sox and one of my longtime teammates, down there with me, because he was going through some difficult times.

They were always checking on Hoffy to see how he was doing. We got very close and we did a lot of talking. It was more of a mental thing with him. We'd spend most of our time talking, instead of working out. He just had a meltdown. It was very sad to see because he was such a nice guy and I loved him. I tried to do the most I could possibly do to help him out. I think the pressure of Boston was a little bit too much for him.

He was down there with me for quite some time. As a matter of fact, one time they sent me home from coaching just to be with him. We would work out in one of my neighbor's batting cages, and we'd end up hitting 10 balls and talking for a half hour. I was kind of like his psychiatrist.

It was kind of weird, but I loved him so much that I'd do anything for him. He's a sweet guy and he's spent years as a successful coach for the Dodgers and Padres. He's just one of the best people I've ever been around in this game.

CHAPTER 4
AH, FENWAY

For me, Fenway feels like a second home. As a kid growing up in Massachusetts, not all of the games were on TV, but we listened to them on the radio with my grandfather hoping someday I'd be able to go to Fenway Park.

I believe I was nine years old the first time I set foot in Fenway. I remember walking up to that runway between home plate and first base and the first thing that hit me was the Monster and the color, that green color. It was just amazing.

The Red Sox were taking batting practice and you saw the Green Monster, the green grass, and you saw the colors of the uniforms, which really stood out to me. My memory is forever ingrained with the red piping and the red-white-and-blue socks they wore in those days. It's a memory that I'll never forget.

Our family used to go to the games quite often because in those days you could walk up and get really good seats. Personally, I used to hope that we'd get to go to a doubleheader. I remember when we did get to go to one, the lights would come on at some point right before it got dark. I had chills just being there because as a kid, the Red Sox were something you listened to and something you saw on TV. Being there was like an out-of-body experience.

I remember driving up from Somerset, up Route 24, and you would finally get to that Braintree split. I used to start looking for the lights not realizing that you couldn't see them until you were about a block away. Every ballpark I'd go by and saw lights I would say, "Is that Fenway?" And my father would say no, my grandfather would say no. We'd continue on and I must have said this four or five times before we actually got there. Then when you get there, it's in this little neighborhood and it was stunning to me to see the light towers. I can remember it like it was yesterday, and to be honest I've never really lost that feeling of the first time I ever saw Fenway in person.

I still get the same feeling as I drive in now, even though I come in from a different direction. But I always take a peek when I get to the Mass Pike and you look at the city and you say, "I'm going there."

It has a very special place in my heart because my love has always been baseball and my love has always been the Red Sox and my love has always been Fenway Park.

This is the most unique sports venue in the world. Look around the ballpark. There's a triangle in center field. There's the red seat in the right field bleachers where Ted Williams hit that 502-foot home run, the longest in Red Sox history. I always got a kick out of David Ortiz and Mo Vaughn, both of whom hit monster homers with their incredible left-handed power, questioning how anyone could hit one anywhere near that seat.

There's Pesky's Pole down the right-field line. There's still a ladder on the Wall. There's Canvas Alley. There's a Green Monster and now there are Monster Seats. The place is so unique.

I think that's why when there was talk about a new Fenway by the Yawkey ownership, it was met with quite a bit of resistance from Save Fenway groups that wanted no part of a new place.

When the Henry/Werner/Lucchino group came in, I know Larry Lucchino tried to have a new ballpark built. After all, that's what he was known for after building Camden Yards in Baltimore and Petco Park in San Diego. But he found out very quickly, first of all, how difficult it was a get a ballpark approved in Boston. The Patriots had tried hard to build a stadium in Boston and it got so frustrating for them they had to build it in Foxborough.

The fondest memories of players and games for me was watching Pedro Martinez pitch. Those weren't just regular baseball games, those were events. It was like a heavyweight championship fight and I used to look forward to every fifth day as a broadcaster when he pitched because he totally changed the atmosphere of the whole ballpark just by being Pedro. You could sense it.

As a player you can feel the intensity at Fenway. There were times when we weren't playing well, and we didn't really want to come home because we knew they were kind of waiting on us and they'd let us have it. It was almost like we'd be better off staying on the road, so we could win a few games before we went back home. In those days it was a little bit dead because they didn't have the music they have now. It was kind of a quiet place to be until something happened, whether it be bad or good. If it was bad, they would boo. If it was good, they would clap.

But when Pedro pitched you could see the Dominican flags waving everywhere in the ballpark. They started hanging the K signs in center field. It was electric in there and Pedro knew it. He played to the crowd. He gave them every reason to cheer and support him. He loved them, and they loved him. It was a love affair between the fans and Pedro like I'd never witnessed before.

There were a lot of players over the years who the fans loved, from Tony Conigliaro to Carl Yastrzemski to David Ortiz and Manny Ramirez and Roger Clemens. But how this crowd responded to Pedro was like nothing I'd ever seen. He started filling the ballpark. He started making Fenway a tough ticket because the Red Sox started selling out every game. It became fashionable to go to a Red Sox game, and good luck getting a ticket for a Red Sox game when Pedro was pitching.

It had a totally different feel compared to when I played. The first time I played was in a sandlot tournament. Red Sox Hall of Famer Frank Malzone was my manager and it was the first time I got a chance to play on the field. I played shortstop then. I remember I couldn't understand a word Frank was saying because he was chewing tobacco and he was hard to understand anyway. But I was sitting at Fenway Park, Malzone, one of the greatest players in Red Sox history was my manager, and I was playing on this field! I couldn't believe it.

In those days you could see the park was getting old and run down. It was strictly baseball because there were no amenities to speak of. I don't think it was really special to a lot of people back then, but it has definitely become that now. Today it's a tourist attraction and the Henry ownership has put so much money into the ballpark to modernize it yet preserve the wonderful things that we all love about it.

Adding the Monster seats was an incredible idea. That was the work of Janet Marie Smith, a fantastic architect who built Camden Yards and Petco Park and also refurbished Dodgers Stadium. There's a whole different vibe in the ballpark now prior to the games, during games, after games.

One of the greatest events I ever saw there was the 1999 All-Star Game. Because the All-Star Game is a national event, we didn't broadcast the game, but I watched it. Pedro was amazing in that game. Here he was, pitching at Fenway Park, and he's pitching against the steroid team on the other side and he just wanted to make them look silly, and he obviously did make them look silly.

Martinez's strikeout victims included Barry Larkin, Larry Walker, and Sammy Sosa in the first inning and Mark McGwire and Jeff Bagwell in the second inning. But I will say this: after that amazing performance, I felt like Pedro was never quite the same. I think he started to have a few arm issues after that. I know he just wanted to make that National League lineup in the steroid era obviously look like a bunch of fools and he did.

A game I was at as a kid was the day before the final game in 1967, when the Red Sox beat the Twins. Rumor has it I was there the last day when they clinched the American League pennant, but

I wasn't. The rumors had me running on the field and all that but that wasn't the case at all—I watched that one on TV—but I was there the day before, sitting in right field because those were the only tickets we could get, and that was pretty special.

That 1967 finale against the Twins was a memorable game for Fenway. Rico Petrocelli secured the final out of the 5–3 win by catching a pop-up from the Twins' Rich Rollins and the ballpark went nuts. Fans flooded the field and hugged and grabbed the players. It was a scene you'd never see today with top security everywhere. I know a lot of people claimed they were there, but it was truly a blissful moment for any kid who grew up loving this team.

There were other great moments at Fenway.

Fisk's iconic Game 6 home run in the 1975 World Series will forever be in the minds of Red Sox fans. It's the bottom of the 12th and Fisk hit a ball high and close to the left-field line. Fisk is standing near home plate waving the ball fair with his arms and then it's determined that it's a fair ball and the ballpark goes nuts.

Also, Roger Clemens' 20-strikeout game against the Seattle Mariners on April 29, 1986. Clemens was so dominating. He didn't walk a batter. It was a chilly night at the ballpark and there were only 14,000 people in the stands. The Celtics were playing an important playoff game at Boston Garden that night and the focus of the Boston sports fan was mostly on that game, Larry Bird vs. Dominque Wilkins.

Roger allowed three hits and one run, a solo homer by Gorman Thomas in a 3–1 Red Sox win. He won the first of his seven Cy Young awards that season.

There were obviously a lot of Ted Williams moments, but two stick out even though I've only read about them. One was the July 9, 1946, All-Star Game, when the game really meant something. Williams went 4-for-4 with a home run, four runs scored, five RBIs, and a walk.

And then his farewell game on September 28, 1960. He ended his career with his 521st home run. At the tender age of 41, he hit .316 with a 1.096 OPS.

Of course, 1967 will always be special for me, because that's when I think Red Sox fans became true Red Sox fans. That didn't even happen during the Williams era, as great as Ted was, and being the greatest hitter who ever lived, not many people came to the ballpark to watch him. But '67 captured a whole generation of Red Sox fans.

Ted Williams crosses the plate after hitting a home run in his last game on September 28, 1960. (AP Images)

That team, comprised of homegrown players, was the team that made us all Red Sox fans for life. And anyone in their 50s, 60s, and 70s knows what I mean. In the 1967 World Series, teachers would bring the black-and-white TV to their classes so the kids could watch the start of the games before they were dismissed. That's how much everyone was involved. Of course, back then the games were in the daytime, and kids got to watch and really get into the team.

Playing at Fenway for me was a challenge because I was a left-handed hitter and I didn't have enough power to use the wall in left field to my advantage, so they could play me shallow and take base hits away. Whereas Yankee Stadium was much bigger in left field, so they had to play you honest—if the ball goes by them you're talking about extra bases, which is why I always enjoyed playing there more than I did at Fenway as it suited my style a little bit better. But for guys like Wade Boggs and Yaz and Fred who could hit the left-field wall, it was heaven. I've always said that Fenway was built for a left-handed hitter who could hit the ball the other way and get some really cheap hits.

Mechanically it keeps you on target because if you're shooting for the opposite field it means your head and shoulder are on the ball, so it's a paradise for left-handed hitters, not for home run hitters. If you're pulling the ball because it's so deep out to the bullpens in right field, it can put you in some deep slumps.

In my opinion, Boggs was the best Fenway hitter. He had the strength and the ability to flip it off the wall any time he wanted to, and he could pull the ball for base hits. He could hit it up the middle. I think Lynn used it very well, too.

Manny Ramirez was one of the best hitters I've ever seen. He could hit anywhere, but he used Fenway to his advantage. He was dumb like a fox and he was so smart hitting-wise that he'd set pitchers up. They'd throw him a curve and he'd duck out of the way and then he'd just sit there and look for another curve because he was baiting the pitcher into throwing him another one. When he got it, he'd just absolutely mash it.

Now, I can't say Manny played the best left field at Fenway. There were times you'd look out there and he'd be 20 feet behind the infield. I've always been a proponent of playing shallow in left field here because a ball over your head is only going to be a double anyway and you can take away base hits, but it'd get to a point where we'd look out there sometimes and he's 25 feet behind the shortstop. It was unbelievable.

When you're there every day, there are things you take for granted. The sellout streak, 820 games, the longest in major sports history, ended on April 10, 2013, when the official attendance in an 8–5 loss to Baltimore was 30,862. A sellout for a Fenway night game is 37,493.

The streak began in May of 2003 and included the postseason. The streak broke the record previously held by the Portland Trail Blazers from 1977 to 1995. We also held the regular season record of 794 sellouts, which surpassed the previous high by the Cleveland Indians of 455 games, set by that team from 1995 to 2001.

It was a pretty big deal when it finally ended. But it was understandable after the horrible 2012 season where fans were upset about the direction of the team. Of course, 2013 turned out to be a great season, a World Series championship season. I think this was almost like pushing the reset button with the fan base, who after the 2011 collapse and the last-place 2012 team was looking for a reason to believe again.

The atmosphere in those days was just over-the-top excitement. Everyone wanted Red Sox tickets. Everyone wanted a chance to go to Fenway Park.

Fenway is also home for "Sweet Caroline," which is played before the bottom of the eighth inning and is probably the most popular time at Fenway Park on a daily basis. The *Boston Globe* wrote that when the song was first played at the park, it was only during random games, between the middle of the seventh and ninth innings, and it was only played if the Red Sox were ahead in the game.

But that changed when a Red Sox employee, Amy Toby, saw that the song was a good luck charm and, in 2002, "Sweet Caroline" became an official Fenway tradition. To this day, the song is played before the bottom of the eighth inning at every home game. It's also played at Jet Blue Park in Fort Myers, Florida, the spring training home of the Red Sox where Jet Blue Park is a Fenway replica complete with a Green Monster wall and Monster seats.

CHAPTER 5
WHO DID IT BEST?

Carlton Fisk and Jason Varitek

Obviously, I knew Carlton Fisk better than Jason Varitek. I played with Fisk and I covered Varitek. They're both very similar in their competitive ways though they acted quite differently. Fisk, a Hall of Famer, was kind of laid-back. Nothing seemed to get him stirred up except the Yankees, who we absolutely hated. One of the funny stories when I got traded to the Red Sox involved Mickey Rivers, who was a former Angels teammate of mine. At the time Mickey was a Yankee. We were warming up before infield practice in those days and Rivers came up to me to shake my hand and just chat. Fisk saw that, and he came over to me right away. He said, "We don't talk to those bastards around here." I kinda got an introduction on how he felt about New York in that little session. That was good enough for me. Once we got playing in the game, I kind of figured out why.

Fisk was very methodical in everything he did. On the field, he took his time getting into the batter's box. Off the field, he could be the same way. Fisk, Fred Lynn, and I used to live in the same development and would carpool together to the ballpark. We'd have a 2:00 PM meeting time to leave for the ballpark. Fred and I would go over to his house and he'd just be sitting down to have dinner at 2:00. He was one of those guys where it seemed like nothing bothered him. But he was very, very competitive in his own way. Probably the best catcher I ever played with or against.

What made him unique was the fact that he was so big. He was 6-foot-3, which was unusually tall for catchers back in those days. Quite frankly, it's unusual in today's game. It was amazing the things that he was able to do. We used to call him "Magic" because of the way he could handle a glove. He was so good handling the glove behind the plate. He played in a time when they didn't have the information that's available to players nowadays. Pretty much everything you did as far as setting up hitters and knowing hitters' tendencies was based on your own memory and feel for the game.

He wasn't afraid to go out to the mound to chew out a pitcher. It would take him a while to get out there, but once he finally did, he could let him have it pretty good. His throws to second base were like arrows. They were just straight. There was no tail on them. There was no nothing. He threw it directly over the top. He was a pretty special guy to play with. And he was a good friend.

We maintain a good relationship to this day. Every time that he stops in a luxury box up in Fenway, he says hi. I've gotten to know his family very well from living in the same development with him. It was kind of a close relationship. Obviously, you go separate ways when you're done playing. The shame of it all is that he never should have left the Red Sox. He should've been in Boston his whole career. I remember the night before they didn't issue his contract. He called me and said, "You're not gonna believe this but tomorrow's the deadline and I don't have my contract yet."

I said, "What?" I couldn't believe it. He couldn't believe it either.

He was a very stubborn guy, very stubborn. His wife, Linda, was very strong. She was his backbone. Once they didn't receive the contract, all hell broke loose. Next thing you know, he's playing with the Chicago White Sox, which should've never happened. He was from New England, from New Hampshire, he was popular, he was good, a Hall of Famer. All of a sudden, he's playing for the Chicago White Sox, where he played more games than he did with the Red Sox. It was really kind of bizarre when that started to happen.

That was the beginning of the breaking up of what was a really good team. After that, Burleson left to go to the Angels. Fred left. They got rid of all the core guys. I stayed because I had a contract. We thought from '78 on we could've gone on and won maybe a couple of championships with that club. All of a sudden, the base of

Carlton Fisk's famous home run in Game 6 of the 1975 World Series. (AP Images)

it really changed because of those moves. That was kind of tough to swallow at that time. You see great players going to other ballclubs. The club was not the same club as what we had. Fisk was a major factor in that. They had a very difficult time replacing him behind the plate. He was a Hall of Famer.

Our scouts would go out prior to a series. If we were playing the Yankees, they would go see the Yankees before we see them. All we had were written reports from our advance scout that were nowhere near as detailed as what they have now or even in Varitek's time with the Red Sox. We'd have these meetings before the games and the manager would come out and say, "Okay, this guy's swinging the bat good. This guy's not swinging the bat good. This guy will hit and run. This guy will do that." It was stuff like that. It was usually before we saw a club for the first time. Information was not very solid. Most of the time, the scouts didn't see the pitchers we were going to see in our series. We had no idea what these guys were doing, how they were throwing. Most of it, in those days, was just based on memory. It was what you remembered about a particular guy. What you remembered he hit against you and where he hit the ball.

They did have pitchers meetings but they weren't nearly as detailed as they are now. There wasn't a real game plan going in. It was just pretty much based on what we've seen in the past and what our recollection was. From a catcher's point of view, that had to be very difficult because he wasn't loaded with the information about how they were doing or how they were swinging at that particular time.

Well, Fisk had an interesting relationship with pitchers. He'd put down some fingers and they'd shake 'em up. Next thing you know, the mask was on top of the head and he was walking out to the mound. There's plenty of famous pictures of him walking out to the mound. That's when sometimes you get pretty intense out there.

It was a general back and forth between him and the pitchers. I think he butted heads with Bill Lee quite a bit on things that they wanted to do.

The thing that amazes me is the knowledge that he had about hitters despite having limited information to work with. It was pretty much a field game at that time. How things were going in that particular game, how things had developed since the last time we saw 'em. You see a team in May, but you don't see them again until August. Things change. Fisk had to figure most of that out on his own. That was quite different from Jason's time, where I remember seeing him sitting at his locker just studying charts of pitchers and hitters. He was a real student and pored over the information.

Jason looked more like a catcher than Fisk. He was built like a rock. He had tree trunks for legs. He was great at blocking the plate. It was very dangerous for him, but it was like hitting a stone wall when you hit him. With Fisk, he had blown out his knee early in his career and it was at a time when surgeries were experimental. It is amazing that they were able to fix his knee and he was able to have the lengthy career that he had. That was really pretty remarkable. He was a little bit more hesitant than Varitek on blocking the plate because of that knee problem. Varitek would just stick a leg out and it was like hitting a tree trunk. They were different in those ways.

Varitek reminded me more of Munson's body shape than Fisk did. Fisk just didn't look like a catcher. He was so big. They were both fiercely competitive. Varitek was quiet. He was not a guy who went around and chatted a lot in the clubhouse, but he was always open to talking to pitchers. He was very up-to-date with knowledge and information that was presented to him. Both were looked up to by everybody on the team just because of the way they played the game. Jason wasn't a rah-rah guy who went around cheering people on and picking guys up. He said what he had to say and what he had to say meant a lot to a lot of players.

Jason had a strong relationship with everyone, but he was definitely known as Pedro's catcher. Pedro trusted him completely. He knew he'd put down the right fingers. Pitchers knew he had a game plan. I think that impressed them, knowing that this guy has an attack in mind and this is the way we're going to go about it. I don't think many of them questioned him very often.

For a pitcher to have confidence in his catcher is one of the most important relationships on the field. When you're sitting out there and you're playing a game and your pitcher and catcher are

Jason Varitek had the confidence of all the Red Sox pitchers during his career in Boston, including closer Jonathan Papelbon. (AP Images)

not on the same page, it doesn't work. It just doesn't work. When they're not on the same page, there's so much time spent going out to discuss pitches. It's disruptive. When you have confidence in the catcher, you know he's putting down the right fingers. It also gives the pitcher confidence. This guy knows exactly what he wants me to do, now I've got to execute it. This is the best chance we have of getting people out.

That was Varitek's strength, in my opinion, that he knew exactly what he wanted to do. It took a lot of convincing to change his mind. I think he also had a very good feel for each individual pitcher on what their strengths and weaknesses were on that particular day. I think he read very quickly that, "Well, today he doesn't have his good breaking ball so we're gonna go to a plan B." I think he was very good changing up midstream depending on what the pitcher had that particular day.

Pedro Martinez and Roger Clemens

I was lucky to see both Pedro Martinez and Roger Clemens up close. I actually played a couple of games behind Roger but most of it was broadcasting his games. They were two guys who desperately wanted to be the best in the game but had totally different styles.

Roger was more of a workaholic. He worked very hard at keeping himself in shape. He was intimidating. He'd buzz you in a second. He was kind of old school. He grew up idolizing Nolan Ryan and he had that kind of stuff. He was amazing to watch. I mean, a blazing fastball, a great split-fingered fastball. You watched him grow and grow as a pitcher. Then he became, obviously, an elite pitcher. I was lucky enough to do his second 20-strikeout game against Detroit on September 18, 1996. It was a pretty amazing feat. I didn't see the first one (on April 29, 1986), but to sit there and broadcast a game like that, wow! As a hitter you had no chance. If he had his stuff and he was on, he was devastating to face. He put that fear in hitters that other great pitchers had. I remember he struck out Travis Fryman four times including the final out of the game, and Tony Clark three times. Alan Trammell and Brad Ausmus were the only regulars who struck out only once. Roger threw 151 pitches in that game and I just can't imagine any pitcher staying out there that long nowadays. The other amazing thing was that he didn't walk anyone, just as he had done in his first 20-strikeout game 10 years earlier. That was Roger's last year with the Red Sox as the Red Sox made what was likely an unwise choice not to re-sign him.

He did whatever it took to be a winning pitcher, to be a winner in any particular game. Even on the days where he didn't have his best stuff, he was still able to survive because he was Roger Clemens. When they let him go, I wasn't against it. I thought that he needed a jumpstart in his career at that time. I thought that he was motivated to become what he was after he left the Red Sox. I think that leaving pissed him off to no end and he couldn't believe that had happened. He said, "Well, screw you guys. I'm gonna show you." Did he ever.

All the great athletes are like that. They find some type of motivation. I honestly believe that he thought he'd be with the Red Sox his whole career. I think that sometimes when you get in those situations, you get a little bit stale. That might sound harsh, but I think he was a little bit stale here. I think that by moving on, going to another club, he got his fire back. And when he got his fire back, look out. We all know what he did. He was special.

But I must say I list him at number two on my list. Pedro is number one.

Pedro was the best I've ever seen. For a lot of reasons, but mostly his pitching ability. He's another guy who had a chip on his shoulder because the Dodgers told him that he couldn't be a starting pitcher.

He was too small. He never forgot about that, both in Montreal and when he came to Boston. He was electric. It was something like we've never seen around here. The ballpark turned into a World Series game every time he pitched. He created that. He's another guy that was mean like Roger was, but in a different way.

Roger was just big, strong, and mean. Pedro was this little guy who could throw 98 miles an hour with a devastating change-up. One that you knew was coming and you still couldn't hit it.

Both Pedro and Roger had great stuff, but I'd say Pedro had a better off-speed pitch. Roger had that split, which was pretty devastating. Pedro's change-up was the best I've ever seen. I honestly believe he could walk up to home plate and tell you, "I'm gonna throw you four change-ups in a row." And you couldn't hit them. He had the same mentality as Roger. He was going to be the intimidator out there. He wasn't afraid to buzz people, as we saw on many occasions. He honestly believed that was part of pitching. I agree with both of them that intimidation is part of pitching. When you've got a hitter who's not quite sure what a pitcher is going to do, that's intimidating. That's a quality that they both shared. Pedro is my all-time favorite. I couldn't wait as a broadcaster to do his games every five days. I just couldn't wait because it was like a heavyweight fight. It would have that kind of an atmosphere at the ballpark every time that he took the mound.

My favorite Pedro game actually wasn't at Fenway. It was the one at Yankee Stadium on September 10, 1999, when he struck out 17 Yankees. He gave up a second-inning home run to Chili Davis early in the game and then they couldn't touch him. It was the only hit he allowed. He retired 22 straight batters, struck out the side in the fifth, seventh, and ninth innings. He embarrassed them the rest of the way. It got so bad that Yankees fans were cheering for strike-outs. And the Yankees were in first place at the time. I mean, he just

The one and only Pedro Martinez. (AP Images)

basically embarrassed them the rest of the way. That was better than some no-hitters that I've seen.

In fact, that's probably the best game that I've ever seen pitched. Believe me, I've been behind no-hitters, I've broadcast no-hitters. I've never seen a game like that. I've never broadcast a game like that. His personality was so different. He was such a clown, really. A smart clown in the clubhouse. He was much better with the media than Roger was. Roger was uncomfortable with reporters. Pedro was totally comfortable with them. He'd say some things that were just absolutely hilarious, like, "Babe Ruth can kiss my ass." Or whatever it was. Stuff like that. He was a pleasure to cover. He was a real quality guy. He goes down in my book as the best pitcher that I've ever seen. I've never had to face him, obviously. I do believe that after that incredible performance in the 1999 All-Star Game, he was never the same. I think that he just wanted to embarrass people in that game and he did. It was at Fenway Park. I think that after that, I don't know if physically he was ever quite the same as he was prior to that game.

Both Roger and Pedro were accused of kind of being on their own schedule. But that's not unusual. When you're a superstar, as long as you're getting your work done, I think managers can tolerate it. They both got their work done. I played with Nolan Ryan. He was on his own schedule, too. He also worked extremely hard, as both these guys did.

I think the only time Pedro did something wrong was he got to the park late and Jimy Williams didn't start him in a playoff game against the Indians. Pedro was never a guy who got to the park early on days that he pitched. Now, I couldn't say what time he'd get there because I was not in the clubhouse at the time. All we knew is that we were sitting there waiting for Pedro to pitch and then the next thing you know, he's going back up the runway. We had no clue what was going on. We found out later, obviously, that Jimy was tired of him being late. That didn't sit very well with Pedro or probably with the 34,000 fans who were waiting for him to pitch.

I think that strained the relationship between Pedro and Jimy. From a manager's point of view, it was something he felt like he had to do to set an example for everybody else. From Pedro's point of view, he knew he was ready to pitch. I'd say that stuff happened more in the older days than it does today. If they got their work done and they performed, nobody would say anything. That's just the way it was. Both of these guys were pretty much on their own routines. They were hard workers. Roger was as hard a worker as you find. Pedro was the same way. Everybody gets ready for their games and their seasons differently. There's not one set routine that works for everybody. As they matured into great pitchers, they figured out what worked for them and what didn't work for them.

Obviously with Roger there's the issue of PEDs that hangs over his head to this day. But I think he belongs in the Hall of Fame. I can't answer for a lot of these guys. I think as time goes on, I think they're all going to probably end up being in there. I think that Hall of Fame voters are putting the PED stigma aside more and more. It was a bad era. There's no question about that. If one guy's on it, others felt like they had to be on it, too, to compete. Believe me, I can tell you this, had that stuff been available back when I played, there'd have been plenty of guys on it. In our era, we had amphetamines. You took whatever would give you the edge in a particular game. Had that stuff been available, I think anybody who tells you they wouldn't have done it is lying. I think that they would've done it to help get an edge.

As time goes by, I think it's going to become an era of baseball that's not looked upon as a great one but these are all great players. They were all great players without the stuff. I don't care what generation you come from, anything that could give you an edge you were going to take. In their case, it happened to be steroids.

Jim Rice and Ted Williams

The other big Boston Red Sox position has traditionally been left field. Obviously, there was Ted Williams, the greatest Red Sox player ever. I was too young to remember Williams. I saw Yaz and obviously I played with Jim Rice. Yaz was my favorite, of course. As a teenager growing up, he was like my idol. He's the guy who in '67 brought baseball back to Boston, with that particular team going from last place to first place under Dick Williams and of course Yaz being the Triple Crown winner and the MVP. It was like Yazmania in Boston. Everybody was crazy about Yaz. Good for him, because he played on some lousy teams. I think he always played in the shadow of Williams. That year really brought him to the forefront. People realized how good a player he was. I think people around baseball knew, but I don't think a lot of the fans realized it. They finally saw it all come together in '67.

He was the guy everybody emulated. Any kid who had a left-handed swing held the bat like Yaz. I was the same way. I was fortunate enough to get a chance to play with him toward the end of his career and got to be there for all those great moments, like when he got his 3,000th hit with his 500th home run. When he retired in 1983, I said, "Well, there's the end of the Red Sox." For me, the Red Sox were always about Yaz. It was a weird feeling that last weekend when he was gone.

He told me in spring training of 1983 that he was going to retire at the end of the year. I never thought he was going to go. My locker was right next to his in Winter Haven, Florida. I said, "You've still got plenty left in the tank." He disagreed. He made up his mind and that was it. It was a wonderful opportunity for me to get to know him and to play with him for a brief period of time.

I never met a guy who worked as hard at hitting as he did. If he had a bad game, he'd make our groundskeeper Joe Mooney pull that cage out after the game and go out there and hit for hours. People didn't see a lot of that. He spent hours and hours in the cage prior to the game with Walt Hriniak. He just cared about hitting. At that point in his career he had done everything defensively in the outfield, winning seven Gold Gloves. He'd done all that. He was now playing some first base. What he cared about was hitting.

One thing that he didn't want to do was miss a fastball. He didn't want to be late. He had all kinds of different stances at the end where it was kind of funny at times. The only fastball I saw him miss was his last at-bat at Fenway when, I think it was Dan Spillner, if I'm not mistaken, threw a quickie right down the middle for him but he threw it too slow. Yaz popped it up. That was his final at-bat at Fenway Park. You knew the guy was just going to groove one, but he threw it too damn slow. Yaz was out in front. It was funny to watch but we were all pulling for a home run there. Obviously, it didn't happen. He was my guy. He was the guy. He was the man to me.

He was also a fierce competitor. He was mentally tough, very tough. He wasn't the easiest guy to get to know but once you got to know him he was your friend for life. He was another guy who wasn't a rah-rah guy in the clubhouse. He was pretty much a loner. He had his circle of friends. He was another leader by example. You didn't see a lot of his work ethic. He didn't care if people saw it. He didn't care about stuff like that.

I didn't know what to expect when I met him the first time. I was with the Angels. There was no conversation. Strength training, drills, he didn't give a shit about any of that. He cared about hitting. Even today I have to laugh, because we were in spring training in

2018 and he comes over to the big-league field every once in a while. He's sitting there and they're going through all the fundamentals and the drills and the pitchers covering first. He goes, "All right. Enough of this shit. Let's hit." That's kind of the way he thought all the time.

Both he and Ted were spring training hitting instructors, but I never knew how close Yaz and Ted were. They obviously had a relationship, but I can't say it was buddy-buddy. I don't know if anybody was real close to Ted. Ted was Ted. The first time I saw Ted Williams, he walked into the clubhouse in Winter Haven and walked by the mirror near the bathroom right in the middle of the locker room. He put his arms out and he goes, "There he is. The greatest hitter of all time." And then just walked away. Yaz kind of looked at me like, "OMG." I think a lot of the uncomfortableness came from Yaz having to live in the shadow of this big, boisterous, great player, Ted Williams, who was the face of the organization. I'm not so sure Yaz ever got over that. I don't know. That's something he'd have to answer. That's just my impression of it. I don't think they disliked each other. But I don't think they were the best of friends, either.

Jim Rice is great man, a Hall of Famer. This guy played every single day. In 1978 he played 163 games because of the tie-breaker game vs. the Yankees. Jimmy was quiet. He had a rocky relationship with the media. All he wanted to do was play baseball. He didn't want to deal with anything but baseball. Another guy who wasn't a clubhouse leader or a chat-'em-up kind of guy. He just came in, put his uniform on every day, and played his ass off. There were days that he should've never been playing but he played. He played all the time.

He was a little difficult to get to know. I got to know him, and I get along very, very well with him. I think there was some jealousy between him and Fred Lynn. They were called the Gold Dust Twins when they came up in 1975 and Fred wound up winning the Rookie of the Year and the MVP of the American League, while Jimmy also had a great season but suffered a broken hand in September. I think that bothered him a lot. I really do. I can't say that he and Fred were close. I think Jimmy tolerated him. Jimmy's a different guy now than he was when he played. He's much more talkative now. He's much

Terry Francona, Jim Rice, and I at an event in 2008. (AP Images)

friendlier. I really believe that the big thing that was lifted off his shoulder was when he got into the Hall of Fame. I've noticed a difference in him: his personality, his style, his friendliness. I think he went all those years not believing that he was getting into the Hall of Fame. Then he finally got in on his 15th and final year of eligibility. It was like taking a load off his shoulders.

I remember doing an interview with him the day that he got elected and he was ecstatic. I've never seen him so happy in my life. He learned how to play the Green Monster. He played it great. In 1978, he was the best player in the league. He just did everything for us. We knew when he came to the plate that he was going to be the guy and he was going to get it done. You just had so much confidence in him.

For some reason, we hit it off. I don't know why. I have no idea why. I think he liked the way I played. I think he liked the way I went about my business. He liked me. To this day, we get along terrific.

He was naturally strong. He was the kind of guy that when we went down to take physicals prior to the season, he wouldn't even bother. He'd just go out there and play. That's all he wanted to do. All this other crap that we did, he didn't want any part of that stuff. I don't think he ever lifted a weight in his life. He was pretty special. I can't rank these guys. It was just a pleasure for me to be on the same team with both those guys, Yaz and Jimmy, to watch how both of them went about their business.

Rice was a lot like J.D. Martinez—power the other way. He wasn't the same type of hitter as J.D., who was more of an inside-out hitter. Jimmy was more of a wrist hitter. He'd flip those wrists and he's so strong it would just be a flick of the wrist and boom, the ball would go miles. A lot of times, Jimmy's hits to the opposite field were a mistake to him. He was so damn strong that he'd get jammed and he'd hit a line drive to the opposite field. J.D. is more of an inside-out hitter thinking the opposite field. I'm not sure Jim thought that way. I think a lot of his ability was just natural ability. His wrists were so strong and so quick. I think that's how he got things done.

At the end of his career, Jimmy had trouble with his eyes. His eyes were always a problem for him, but as he got older they became more of a problem for him. He was always getting his eyes examined. His decline was fairly rapid, and I think his eyes had a lot to do with it. But not too many guys ever did it better than him. He deserves to be in the Hall of Fame.

CHAPTER 6
2004:
MY FAVORITE
TEAM

My favorite team of all time was the 2004 team. They were a little bit off center, but they did something here that nobody else could ever do—at least not for 86 years. They won it all. They were a great bunch of guys to be around, they were fun, and they enjoyed baseball. Fenway Park and Boston didn't intimidate those guys like a lot of teams get intimidated playing here.

They had so many characters on that club, like Johnny Damon, Kevin Millar, Manny Ramirez, David Ortiz, Pedro Martinez, and Bronson Arroyo. They had really serious guys like Bill Mueller, Mark Bellhorn, Jason Varitek, Trot Nixon, and Curt Schilling. They had a manager in Terry Francona who simply had the right touch and the patience to handle a group like that.

This wasn't a team that breezed through anything. They finished second in the American League East with 98 wins, three games behind the Yankees, who won 101 games. They had to win it all from the wild card position, which meant no home-field advantage. They had to make a major trade at the deadline that year, parting with the beloved Nomar Garciaparra. But the deals that brought back Orlando Cabrera, Doug Mientkiewicz, and Dave Roberts were really the trigger to the remainder of the season which enabled them to win it all.

What's lost is that they swept the Angels in the divisional series in three games. Nobody even mentioned that because what was to come was the most impressive thing I've ever seen in sports. It was a pretty special group because they had the ability, the mental strength to come back from an 0–3 deficit against the Yankees in the ALCS. It was the greatest comeback in sports. At least in my mind it was. You go from really having no hope after you'd lost Game 3 by the score of 19–8 and thinking a sweep was on the way, to feeling the euphoria of coming back to win Game 4. And suddenly you could almost feel the groundswell of a comeback. Oh, c'mon, nobody thought they could win four straight against the Yankees and get to the World Series, but then game after game, win after win, it all just started to fit, and you'd say, "My god, could this really happen?"

I remember doing the postgame show on NESN and saying at that time that if they went on to win the World Series it was going to be the biggest parade anyone had seen in their life, and it was. That parade was just absolutely incredible. I was on a duck boat and the crowd noise was deafening. I don't know how many people were there along the route. I have no clue. But I've never seen anything like that before and likely never will again.

This was a team that kind of bridged generations of people. There were people who lived and died never seeing a Red Sox team win a championship. Think about that. We were indeed cursed. The Curse of the Bambino was real. It lived in all of us. When they finally won it, there were so many heartwarming stories about how an elderly person got to experience a world championship on their deathbed. There were fans who went to the gravesites of their deceased loved ones and put Red Sox banners on them. The night they completed a sweep of the Cardinals in the World Series, there were thousands of people in the streets of Boston just ecstatic over what they had experienced.

I had chills down my spine because I understood so well what this feeling was, not only as a kid growing up here but as a player who experienced the heartbreak of 1978. And just like that team that I thought should've won it all, the 1986 team should have, too, marred by the infamous ball going through Bill Buckner's legs against the Mets in Game 6.

All of that stuff came to everyone's mind on that night. The World Series was almost icing on the cake. It was almost melodramatic because the ALCS was mind-blowing.

The Red Sox had won the season series 11–8, but the Yankees managed to beat Pedro twice in September. It was just one year after Grady Little left Pedro in too long and Aaron Boone hit the walkoff homer against Tim Wakefield to eliminate Boston in the ALCS in seven games.

The Yankees won the first two games at home, again beating Martinez in Game 2, 3–1. Yankees fans were having fun with Pedro's famous "Who's Your Daddy?" quote. The Yankees just pounded us 19–8 in Game 3 at Fenway Park, and there was absolutely no reason to think we'd even win a game much less the series. No team had ever come back from 0–3.

Until this one.

Francona kept telling the guys that all they needed to focus on was the next pitch. So, on October 17, 2004, the historic run began.

The Yankees were ahead 4–3 in the bottom of the ninth. They were about to humiliate and embarrass the "Idiots." The greatest reliever of all time, Mariano Rivera, was on the mound.

Which is why what was about to happen was so special.

It all began when Rivera walked Millar. It was really a great at-bat and very patient of Millar to stay back and see the ball into the mitt. That's when Francona called upon Dave Roberts to come into the game and pinch-run for Millar. Roberts had been a nice trade deadline acquisition for the Red Sox, who needed speed in that lineup. Being a speed guy myself, I watched Roberts closely the rest of the season. He was really an outstanding base runner. I know Dave repeated a line that the great Maury Wills often told him: "There's going to come a time when you have to do something great. You have to put yourself out there and go for it."

This seemed to be that moment.

Rivera threw over to first a few times and Roberts was actually almost picked off once. But Roberts had him sized up pretty well.

David Ortiz's walkoff home run against the Yankees in Game 3 of the 2004 ALCS.

(AP Images)

He took off and just beat Jorge Posada's throw. At the time you thought, "Wow, that was a great play," but it became a greater play considering what it began and what it came to mean.

Mueller singled, driving in Roberts with the tying score and forcing extra innings. With the game about five hours old, Ortiz homered off Paul Quantrill in the bottom of the 12th and it kept the Red Sox alive. Remarkably.

Game 5 was similar to Game 4. Rivera was not on one of his better streaks and blew another 4–3 lead. Roberts again scored, this time on a Jason Varitek sacrifice fly, to tie it up. The game dragged on into the 14th inning. Big Papi was again the hero with a walkoff single against Esteban Loaiza, which scored Damon.

I remember feeling curious about the Yankees' offensive strategy in the eighth inning. They had a 4–2 lead. Miguel Cairo had doubled to lead off the inning against Mike Timlin. Then Derek Jeter bunts him to third. I get trying to advance the runner. But this is Jeter. He's bunting? Alex Rodriguez was up next, so you figure, okay, it's going to be 5–2, but A-Rod didn't do very well in that series. Timlin struck him out and the Yankees didn't score.

Then in the ninth inning of Game 5, I felt the Red Sox got a huge break when Tony Clark hit a ground-rule double into the right-field corner with Ruben Sierra on first. How that ball made it into the stands is beyond me. Even Clark, now the executive director of the players' association, talks about the bad luck the Yankees had. If it hadn't gone over that wall, Sierra would have scored, and New York would have taken the lead.

Even before that, the game showed that baseball is truly a game of inches. Hideki Matsui was up with the bases loaded in the sixth inning of Game 5 and he hit a vicious line drive to right field against Pedro. Nixon caught it, but that could have been three runs for the Yankees if he didn't.

These were absolute nail-biters. It was like sudden death all the time and the Red Sox kept surviving. It was the most suspenseful time I can ever remember in my lifetime. The Sox were down 3–2 and the same sudden-death scenario took hold for Game 6 back at Yankee Stadium.

This was the "Bloody Sock" game. Schilling had a torn tendon sheath in his right ankle. Normally there's no way he could have pitched. But Dr. Bill Morgan and his staff got together and tried to figure out a way they could keep things in place enough for Schilling to pitch. They decided to suture the sheath in place.

Schilling managed to pitch pretty well. You could see the blood through his right sock. But the Sox gave him a boost when they took a 4–0 lead in the fourth on Bellhorn's three-run homer. Schilling pitched seven innings and the Red Sox won 4–2.

The series was tied at 3–3. The New York newspapers were starting to write about the Yankees choking. The Red Sox had come so far, but was it too far to complete the journey? The Yankees had to win sometime, didn't they?

Well, the Red Sox soon got their answer. Ortiz blasted a two-run homer in the top of the first off Yankees starter Kevin Brown, and Damon blasted a grand slam in the second inning for a 6–0 lead. This was no contest. The Red Sox had overturned a 3–0 Yankees lead in the series with an easy 10–3 win.

Looking back, the Yankees scored 32 runs in winning the first three games against the Red Sox. They scored 19 runs in the third game. How could the Red Sox have been any deader and then how could they have been more alive?

The Red Sox had gotten off to a 15–6 start to start the season. They actually lost their opener with Pedro pitching and Nomar Garciaparra and Trot Nixon injured. But Schilling, who wound up 21–6 (10–3 after Red Sox losses), picked the Sox up in the second half and Keith Foulke started a fine season of 32 saves even after a lousy spring training which was making Red Sox fans nervous.

It wasn't all smooth. They dropped their first five games in May. Mueller made a couple of key throwing errors in a May 4 game in which they allowed five unearned runs. Mueller was playing with a bum knee and he'd have to have surgery and miss part of the season. Despite some concerns about the team defense, Francona called a team meeting and said that he wanted the players to relax and play their game and not worry about errors. Mueller, who had won the batting title, actually responded with a three-run homer in a 9–5 win over the Indians that led to a four-game winning streak.

Nomar had missed the first 57 games with right Achilles tendinitis but he returned on June 9 in an 8–1 loss to the Padres. In that game, more defensive problems reared their ugly head: Bellhorn made two errors and Andy Dominique made one at first base which accounted for five unearned runs. Slick-fielding Pokey Reese was on the bench and the fans were calling for him to come out and save the day.

And it just got worse in the field. They had another bad game against the Phillies. By mid-June they had 54 errors, the most in the majors, and they were only playing .500 ball (26–26) since May 1. While Reese was a big upgrade at shortstop, he hurt his thumb and was very limited. And Mueller had missed about a month with his knee surgery. Theo Epstein started talking about having to do something to help the defense.

One game that really stuck out for me was July 24 against the Yankees, which the Red Sox ended up winning 11–10. The Red Sox had fallen 9.5 games behind the Yankees after losing the night before. The field was really wet, and management wanted to postpone the game, but the players insisted on playing and convinced management to start the game.

It was a big day because there was a lot of emotion from the players. It was the game where Alex Rodriguez got mad after Bronson Arroyo hit him with a pitch and he wanted to fight. Varitek whacked him in the face and it started a bench-clearing brawl. The Sox were losing 10–9 with one out in the ninth when Mueller hit a walkoff two-run homer off Rivera. This really had to be the turning point of the season.

After that, Theo shocked the world. We were in Minnesota at the trade deadline when Theo traded Garciaparra, a two-time batting champion, to the Cubs in a four-team deal that involved eight players. The whole point of the deal was to improve the defense. So, the Red Sox acquired Orlando Cabrera from Montreal. They got Twins first baseman Doug Mientkiewicz, another Gold Glove winner. In a separate deal, they obtained Roberts from the Dodgers, and we know what that led to.

I must admit, it was gutsy to deal Garciaparra. But he wasn't the same player by that point in his career. Injuries had taken their toll. The team's defense was now much improved, because Mientkiewicz could replace Millar defensively late in games and Cabrera was a Gold Glover at shortstop. Roberts improved their team speed and proved to be a guy who could steal a run.

I remember Nomar being sad and somewhat relieved at the same time. He pretty much went up to everyone who covered him in the media and shook their hands and said good-bye. It was a graceful exit. But Nomar's time had come. I think he probably looked back on it and wished he had been part of that championship team at the end. But he was at least there for just over half of the season and had something to do with the World Series win.

It wasn't until August 16 that the Red Sox really took off. They won 20 of their next 22 games and took control of the wild card race and were two games off the division lead behind the Yankees by September 8. But the Sox just didn't have enough to catch them: New York blasted the Red Sox 14–4 and 11–1 in one September series. Francona said afterward, "They put us in the rearview mirror a little bit."

As far as that team goes, Millar was a little bit of a leader because he was so crazy and he's one of those guys where nothing bothered him. He was very outspoken, talking all the time. He and Damon really took the heat off their teammates by always being available to the media. Some thought it was Johnny's team. And he had a very good year. He was a tough guy who played hurt and was the igniter of that offense. He played hard.

Manny was really quiet, but his hitting was devastating. He was just so much fun to watch hit. Every time up, you just wanted to watch how he took apart the pitcher. You knew something good was going to happen when he stepped up to the plate. And David was David. He hit two walkoff homers and a walkoff single in the playoffs. Think about that. Think how clutch, how dramatic one has to be to do something like that. Maybe he wasn't as impactful in the clubhouse as he was later on in his career, but his actions, his dramatics, his feel for the moment was second to none.

We all know what Schilling is like. He's become very political after his playing career. But he's the guy who brought a lot of confidence to every outing he had. When the Red Sox signed him as a free agent that off-season, you could sense that he was going to be a big part of this team after the success he had winning a World Series in Arizona teaming with Randy Johnson. Theo Epstein and his staff did such a great job convincing Schilling to come to Boston on Thanksgiving of that year when they went to his house and convinced him he needed to sign with the Red Sox.

Pedro, of course, was great. He was always great. He kept the media on its toes with some of the great quotes he would give after a game. Things like "I'm gonna hit the Bambino on the ass." He was just fun for all of us and he backed it up with the fabulous pitching that he provided.

They were just a group that didn't care about anything that went on outside those walls. They just believed that they'd go out and win it, even when they were down 0–3 to the Yankees. They didn't think they were going to lose and they turned it into the greatest moment in Red Sox history.

Francona, as I pointed out, was a guy who did everything right. I questioned the hire at the time because he came from a losing organization in Philadelphia. He wasn't successful there and I was kind of surprised that he got the job. But then as you got to know him a little bit you could see why he got the job.

He was a player's manager. He'd be playing cribbage with different players every day. He was a Nervous Nellie. He'd pull players into the office to play cards even when they didn't want to. I always said the shelf life of a manager in Boston is four or five years and then they just get beaten down, and I think it beat him down at the end because of his relationship with the front office. I felt bad for him because he was not a healthy guy and toward the end he was a mess. I think it was kind of a blessing for him that they decided to make a move and go in a different direction. When he got to Cleveland to manage the Indians, he was so much more relaxed and continued to prove what a great manager he is.

Like I said, even though the Cardinals had a great team under Tony La Russa, I just didn't think they had a chance against the Red Sox in the World Series because the momentum was so much in Boston's favor. They were sky-high as a team. So confident. The Cardinals had Albert Pujols in his prime and he had hit 46 home runs and knocked in 123 runs that year. They had a great player in center fielder Jim Edmonds, who hit 42 homers and knocked in 111

89

runs. They had All-Stars up and down their lineup and their pitching staff had allowed the fewest runs in the league.

We were really sloppy in Game 1 at Fenway, committing four errors, but we got off to a great start when Ortiz hit a three-run homer in the four-run first inning. We were ahead 7–2 after three innings, but that lead shrunk to 9–7 heading into the eighth inning. But that was short-lived as Manny's defense reared its ugly head when he made consecutive errors allowing the Cards to tie it 9–9.

But the Cards made a key error of their own in the eighth and Mark Bellhorn, a real unsung hero for the Red Sox that year, homered off the Pesky Pole to make it 11–9. Bellhorn had led the AL in strikeouts with 177 that season. Nowadays that's almost routine for hitters. But he had no trouble connecting. He was also a very good second baseman and one of those quiet guys amid the loud ones.

Schilling took the mound in Game 2 and this was after they had stitched his tendon to his leg in the infamous "Bloody Sock" game of Game 6 in the ALCS. This is where I gained so much respect for him. There was no way Schilling should have been able to last 94 pitches given his condition. But he lasted six innings, struck out four, and held them to four hits and one run. The odd part again is the defense committed four errors, three by the usually sure-handed Bill Mueller. But once again, the Red Sox put aside their defensive problems and got some timely hits with two RBIs from Bellhorn, Orlando Cabrera, and Jason Varitek as the Sox held on for a 6–2 win.

We had won two games at home and now it was on to Busch Stadium where things would get tougher. Except, not really.

Pedro just lit it up with seven scoreless, three-hit innings and the Sox won it 4–1. Jeff Suppan, who had spent some time with the Red Sox, made a base running blunder. He was at third and Edgar Renteria was at second with no outs in the third when Larry Walker hit a grounder toward second base. For some reason Suppan stopped on his way to the plate and returned to third, which forced Renteria to return to second. Bellhorn threw to first to get Walker and Ortiz threw to Mueller at third to retire Suppan! Walker homered off Keith Foulke in the ninth, but it didn't matter, the Series was 3–0, much to the shock of the stunned St. Louis crowd.

The Sox went with Derek Lowe in Game 4. He's a guy who always reminded me of Bob Stanley. He could do anything and did do everything as a Red Sox pitcher, whether it was out of the bullpen or as a starter. He had that heavy sinker and when he was on, he was pretty nasty.

Pedro Martinez, Curt Schilling, and David Ortiz after sweeping the Cardinals in the 2004 World Series. (Getty Images)

He followed up Pedro's great game with one of his own against that tough lineup. He held them to three hits, striking out four in seven scoreless innings. Bronson Arroyo, Alan Embree, and Foulke finished up the 3–0 win and secured a World Series championship. Damon's first-inning leadoff homer was really all the Red Sox needed. After 86 years, the Curse had been lifted. Manny was named the MVP with a .412 average.

The players and their families congregated on the field at Busch while the Cardinals fans watched. Cardinals players were on the bench stunned at what had just happened. The Cardinals had won 105 regular season games that year. La Russa, now a Red Sox executive, often commented that he would walk by the walls in the press box at Fenway and look at a photo of the Cardinals lined up being introduced before Game 1 and wonder, "How did we ever get swept?"

It all worked out well for the Red Sox and their long-suffering fans. It was a tough season, but a beautiful one. One that Red Sox Nation will never forget.

CHAPTER 7
2007

T he incredible thing about this championship team was that the Red Sox led almost from wire to wire. We went up by a half game on April 18 after a 4–1 win over Toronto and we never relinquished the lead. We were in first place for 166 days. We won the division by only two games and there were topsy-turvy times there during the second half of the season, but we never gave it up.

You had to figure this was going to be a special season based on an April 22 game against the Yankees when the Sox hit four consecutive homers—Manny Ramirez, J.D. Drew, Mike Lowell, and Jason Varitek—for the first time in franchise history. The homers came off Yankees starter Chase Wright. The amazing thing is that it was the second time Drew had been part of a four-consecutive-homer situation, the first one coming when he was with the Dodgers on September 18, 2006.

The closest thing to real adversity was going down 3–1 to Cleveland in the ALCS. And then this team pulled off another one of those 2004-type miracles and came back to win the ALCS and got into the World Series against the Rockies and swept them.

A big reason for this success was the December 2005 trade with the Florida Marlins that brought Josh Beckett and Mike Lowell to Boston. It didn't pay off in '06, but a year later when both Beckett and Lowell had a chance to be there for the whole season, they were the pillars of the starting rotation and everyday lineup, respectively.

Beckett was always a terrific talent, but it came shining through in '07. He went 20–7 with a 3.27 ERA with 30 starts and 200⅔ innings. He had 194 strikeouts and only 40 walks. He finished second to CC Sabathia in the Cy Young voting. Lowell hit .324 with 21 homers and 120 RBIs. He also played a terrific third base. He was the "throw-in" in the deal as the Marlins insisted the Red Sox absorb the remainder of the contract, which had two years at $9 million a year. The Red Sox needed a third baseman anyway. They didn't regret paying the money as Lowell also became the World Series MVP against the Rockies.

The Red Sox received some criticism when the trade was made because they gave up highly touted shortstop prospect Hanley Ramirez in the deal. Hanley was a stud, no doubt about it. He was close to a five-tool player who could run, steal bases, hit for power and average. He wasn't a great defensive player. When he got to the Marlins he won the National Rookie of the Year and eventually won a batting title there.

But the deal was worth it. When you give up a young prospect, even if that guy turns out great, if you win a championship with the ones you got back, it's worth it. You have prospects for two reasons—to build with them or to use them for more established talent. That's what the Red Sox did.

Anyway, the weird thing is the deal wasn't even made by Theo Epstein, who had left the team in a dispute with Red Sox CEO Larry Lucchino. Technically it was Lucchino who made the deal with the help of his senior advisers. Ben Cherington and Jed Hoyer were acting GMs at the time, but they hated giving up Hanley.

Theo once said, "You wear rings in October, not in April." And that's how that team approached the entire season.

The 96 wins tied Cleveland for most in the majors. By July 5, the lead was 11.5 games. But the Red Sox just couldn't keep those damn Yankees off their tail. On May 29, they were eight games under .500 and 14½ games behind the Sox. By the last week of the season they were as close as 1½ games, so it got close. But that's about it.

The Angels proved no match for the Red Sox in the ALDS and we swept them in three games.

Beckett was really on his game the whole year. He got us off to a great start when he shut out the Angels 4–0. It got the whole postseason started on the right foot and that's so important in the playoffs, because it just reinforced that great feeling you had in the regular season where you accomplished your first goal in winning the division.

Beckett didn't need much in the way of run support, but Kevin Youkilis got this going with a solo home run in the first inning and then Papi blasted a two-run homer in the third inning. Given Beckett's performance, this one was pretty easy.

In Game 2, both offenses came to life. Through five innings it was 3–3 with Daisuke Matsuzaka and Kelvim Escobar of the Angels matching up. It stayed that way until the ninth when the Red Sox put together the winning rally. Julio Lugo singled and Ortiz walked, setting the stage for Manny Ramirez's walkoff three-run bomb over the Green Monster.

They were up 2–0 and now heading to what at the time was called Angel Stadium of Anaheim. I enjoyed playing there when I played for the Angels. The weather was great all of the time. It was the best baseball weather you could ask for.

The Red Sox loved it. They took the series with a 9–1 win behind Curt Schilling's seven shutout innings. He allowed six hits and struck out four. He was dominating, very impressive with the way he kept the Angels off balance for the entire outing.

Ortiz and Manny, one of the best middle-of-the-order combinations you'll ever see, hit back-to-back homers in the fourth inning. After that they just scorched the Angels bullpen with seven runs in the eighth inning. The Red Sox sweep was one of three Division Series sweeps in the 2007 postseason.

That enabled them to move on to face the Indians in the ALCS.

This series wasn't nearly as easy. In fact, the Red Sox lost three of the first four games and they were on the verge of going home.

The resiliency of this team was surely tested. It was a bunch of guys who always felt confident, as if they had ice water in their veins.

Game 1 was all Red Sox. Beckett again pitched well, and CC Sabathia pitched poorly in a matchup of potential Cy Young winners. After Travis Hafner homered off Beckett in the first and Manny knocked in Kevin Youkilis with a single in the bottom of the first, the Red Sox started to pull away. Lugo started Sabathia's downfall with a ground-rule double. CC then walked Youkilis and hit Ortiz with a pitch, and then Manny walked as the Sox took a 2–1 lead. It got worse. Lowell doubled to score Youkilis. Bobby Kielty walked. When Jason Varitek hit a grounder where the Indians couldn't turn the double play, Ramirez scored. The horse was out of the barn at this point. The Sox scored five more runs to take the 10–3 win.

The roles were reversed in Game 2. The Indians took it 13–6. Curt Schilling just didn't have it. He was gone in the fifth inning but the Sox got to Fausto Carmona to make it a 6–6 game after six innings. This game went into extra innings, but in the 11th, the Sox bullpen was blistered. The trio of Eric Gagne, Javier Lopez, and Jon Lester gave up seven runs.

On to Cleveland, where in Game 3 the Indians continued their run with a 4–2 win. Daisuke Matsuzaka gave up all four Indians runs and Varitek provided the only offense with a two-run homer.

The Sox bullpen was again a negative factor in Game 4. Manny Delcarmen, who had been a mainstay in the Sox bullpen all season, allowed four runs after he relieved Tim Wakefield in the fifth. The Indians scored seven runs in the fifth inning. The Red Sox didn't quit. In the sixth they got three consecutive homers from Youkilis, Ortiz, and Ramirez, but that's about all they could do in a 7–3 loss.

They were faced with a daunting task. They were facing elimination.

Manny made some headlines after this one. Now, Manny avoided the media like nobody else, but he made a comment that resonated nationally when he said, if the Red Sox were eliminated, "It's not like it's the end of the world." You can guess what the media did with that one. The rest of the team was more confident in its ability to come back. All through the clubhouse, there was that feeling that they were capable of turning things around.

While there were rumors about Beckett's back being stiff, he took the mound for Game 5. Beckett showed no signs of discomfort while Youkilis drove in three runs and Ortiz two in a 7–1 win.

Now the series returned to Fenway and there was more reason to believe the players when they said they could do this.

This was the infamous J.D. Drew grand slam game. Drew was really a polished player able to do many things. He was a very good right fielder with a decent arm. He was a good base runner and very good hitter. But he just didn't endear himself with the fan base. He had received a five-year, $70 million deal, and I think fans expected him to be more of a force. He just had that attitude that nothing bothered him and that he came off like he didn't have that great fire.

Schilling pitched better and allowed only two runs in seven innings. He was aided by J.D.'s grand slam in the first inning and the offense exploded for six runs in the third inning. The Sox won it 12–2.

So now all the momentum was in Boston's favor. Dice-K got the ball in Game 7 and allowed just two runs over five innings. Francona turned it over to the bullpen after that with Hideki Okajima and Jonathan Papelbon throwing two innings apiece. They won the game 11–2, fueled by a pair of two-run homers from Dustin Pedroia and Youkilis.

It must be said that the Red Sox pitching really got better under John Farrell. The team had also acquired Matsuzaka through the posting system in Japan, submitting the highest bid of $51.1 million. They also gave Dice-K a six-year, $52 million deal. This was a big deal because Dice-K was the biggest thing out of Japan. He was hugely popular. Known for his famous gyroball, Dice-K brought with him an army of Japanese sportswriters who covered his every movement for a full season. He won 15 games, pitched 204⅔ innings, and struck out 201 batters.

Tim Wakefield, who simply doesn't get enough credit for all he did for this franchise after the Red Sox acquired him off the scrap heap in 1995, won 17 games.

One of the interesting games was watching Schilling come within one out of a no-hitter in Oakland, and the only hit he allowed was after he shook off Jason Varitek. Schilling may have been on the other side of his career, but he managed to learn to pitch with finesse. He went 3–0 in October.

The other memorable game on the pitching front came on September 1 when Clay Buchholz, making only his second major league start, no-hit the Orioles 10–0 at Fenway. That was remarkable to me. I've seen a few no-hitters as a player and broadcaster, but for a rookie to do that? Think about it. The greats like Pedro Martinez and Roger Clemens never pitched a no-hitter, yet this kid throws one in his second start.

I remember there was debate apparently during that game between Terry Francona and Theo Epstein as to whether they needed to take Buchholz out, fearing he was throwing too many pitches. I don't think taking him out would have gone over with the fan base, especially those people who were in the ballpark. Buchholz was simply strong and throwing with ease throughout the game.

Buchholz was pressed into action when the 41-year-old Wakefield came up with a stiff back. The 23-year-old Buchholz got the call.

Pedroia made a great play on a grounder by Miguel Tejeda behind the mound to save the no-hitter. Buchholz struck out nine and walked three. There weren't many other potential hits out there. He put two batters on with walks in the fifth inning, but after that Buchholz was pretty dominant. It was a great kind of sideshow in the middle of a pennant race. The Red Sox, by this time, had gotten some nice contributions from rookies like Pedroia and Jacoby Ellsbury, who came up late in the season and contributed hugely.

The important part of this '07 team was the pitching. The Red Sox were second in the majors with a 3.87 ERA. While Dice-K was doing it in the rotation, Okajima did it from the bullpen as the lefty reliever. He did a great job as a setup man to Papelbon.

Speaking of Papelbon, he had wanted to give starting a try again in spring training, but about halfway through camp, Papelbon realized it wasn't going to work and he went back to the closer role. It was a great decision because he had a great year.

And Francona did a great job managing Papelbon's usage. He wound up saving three of the four World Series games against the Rockies. Papelbon saved 37 games and held opponents to a .146 average. He struck out batters at a rate of 12.97 times per nine innings.

Pap was a little different, but what a competitor. He developed this Irish step dance that he would do, and it was hilarious. He was always ready and he was usually lights-out. It was about as good a performance as I've ever seen from a closer over a full season.

And then there was Ortiz. I give him credit because he played all season with a bad knee. As someone who had 11 knee operations, I sympathized with the task of having to play every day under those conditions. He had hit 54 homers in 2006. You could tell there was something going on because by the All-Star break, David had hit only 14 homers and knocked in 52 runs. That changed in the second half, when I guess the knee started to feel better, and he hit .352 with

21 homers and 65 RBIs. In his last 16 games he hit .441 with seven homers and 19 RBIs. And then in October, he batted .370 with three home runs and 10 RBIs. His 14 walks gave him an on-base percentage of .508. Yes, Papi was back with a vengeance. I think he got sick of hearing what was wrong with him.

Also emerging was Pedroia, the rookie second baseman, who was impressing everyone with the way he played the game. He would win the Rookie of the Year award after hitting .172 as late as May 1. I've got to tell you, I had my doubts about him, but he proved me wrong. What a player.

Youkilis became a heckuva first baseman. No errors all season. He also hit .288 with 16 homers and 83 RBIs. He had a 23-game hitting streak at one point.

Lowell hit .324 with 120 RBIs. For a guy who was supposed to be washed up, he had his best year. He had a great series against the White Sox in August. And he came up biggest in the World Series, where he was named MVP.

Ellsbury, another speedy guy, scored from second base on a wild pitch and hit .438 in the World Series after replacing a slumping Coco Crisp.

One game that really stood out for me was Mother's Day, when we trailed 5–0 and came up with six runs in the bottom of the ninth to win.

Bobby Kielty had a big role in the World Series when he homered in Game 4.

One of the heartwarming stories was Lester, 14 months after his diagnosis of cancer, pitching the World Series clincher. I remember the great photo of Francona going out to embrace him and the look the two gave one another. It was really special.

"What a journey to go from where he was a little more than a year ago," Epstein said after the game about Lester, "to winning the deciding game of the World Series."

Even though the Red Sox swept the Rockies, it wasn't so clear-cut in Boston's favor. The Rockies were the darlings of baseball. They had won 21 out of 22 games, including a one-game wild card playoff against San Diego, to get to the World Series. They swept the Phillies in the NLDS and the Diamondbacks in the NLCS. This team was on an amazing run.

But the Red Sox also had their mojo back after their great comeback against the Indians. Beckett again pitched a gem in Game 1, allowing one run over seven innings. He struck out nine against a very potent Rockies lineup.

Pedroia got the ball rolling when he homered on the second pitch of the game off lefty Jeff Francis. The Red Sox just torched Rockies reliever Franklin Morales for seven runs in the fifth inning and wound up with an easy 13–1 win.

By Game 2 it was becoming obvious the Rockies hadn't experienced this kind of pitching along their journey. Schilling allowed just one run over 5⅓ innings while Okajima and Jonathan Papelbon again teamed to finish off the game in a 2–1 win. Varitek and Lowell drove in runs for all the offense they needed.

Then it was off to Coors Field, where the elevation and air always benefitted the Rockies. But the Red Sox liked the air up there as well. They scored six runs in the third inning. Dice-K helped himself with two RBIs, matching Lowell's production. The Rockies were trying to match the Sox when they scored five, featuring a Matt Holliday homer. But the Sox pulled away on rookies Pedroia and Ellsbury combining for three RBIs in an eventual 10–5 Sox win.

It was hard to believe that the Red Sox could sweep this team and finish them off in their home ballpark, but that's exactly what happened.

Lester got the start with Wakefield down with a bad back. This was a scoreless game into the sixth inning. The Sox went up 2–0 with Ortiz and Varitek driving in the runs. Lowell led off the seventh with a home run and then Kielty hit a pinch-hit home run in the eighth. Okajima allowed a pair of runs but Papelbon closed the door over the final 1⅔ innings to save the victory.

After an 86-year drought, the Red Sox had won two World Series in four seasons. Incredible.

Jonathan Papelbon celebrates getting the final out of the 2007 World Series against the Rockies. (AP Images)

CHAPTER 8
2013

All of the championships were special, but the one in 2013 was emotional. The season started with the Boston Marathon bombings right down the street from Fenway.

We had played our 11:00 AM Patriots' Day game on April 15 and then the team bussed to the airport for a trip to Cleveland.

The players could hear little explosions in the distance as our bus took off for the airport.

Little did we know at the time that terrorists had set off bombs along the marathon route. A huge tragedy was in progress.

The players got to Cleveland and played their series there, all along trying to get together as a team to contribute something in their own way. I think that really brought this group together. They had something to band together over and you just noticed it all season.

The team wore black armbands and there was a banner hanging over the Red Sox dugout with the 617 area code.

We were scheduled to play the Royals back at Fenway on April 19, but the city was on lockdown because they were searching for the bombing suspects. It was just a surreal situation. You saw video on TV of the city and it looked like a ghost town. It was a scary time, but they caught the second suspect in Watertown, not far from the NESN studios.

This was a team like no other I had experienced. General manager Ben Cherington did an absolutely incredible job shaking off the last-place finish of 2012 and trying to regroup the team after the disaster of the Bobby Valentine year.

Cherington brought in manager John Farrell, whom he acquired from the Toronto Blue Jays after he negotiated his release. Cherington brought in several new faces, veterans who had won in other places and who had perhaps not had the best of years in 2012 but hoped they would rebound.

David Ortiz speaking to the fans after the Boston Marathon bombing in 2013. (AP Images)

What a chance he took. He brought in David Ross, a backup catcher in Atlanta. He brought in Shane Victorino, who was not re-signed by the Dodgers. He brought in Ryan Dempster, Stephen Drew, Mike Napoli, Mike Carp, Daniel Nava, Koji Uehara, and Jonny Gomes. And then he traded for Jake Peavy.

My god. How can you have that many new faces and have it all work out?

But it did. Uehara was a tremendous find. He was probably the third closer the Red Sox used because Joel Hanrahan was injured early and underwent Tommy John surgery. Then Andrew Bailey and Andrew Miller both went down with injuries and Uehara, who had been signed as a setup guy, became the closer. And what a run he went on, not to mention he became a fan favorite.

I didn't know what to make of this team for a long time. I didn't know how good they were, but as time went on you could see there was something taking hold. Victorino and Gomes had the flare for the dramatic. Uehara was lights-out. Dempster was a really good back-end starter. Drew did a great job at shortstop and produced some clutch hits. Napoli hit some big home runs and played very well defensively at first base. Jarrod Saltalamacchia hit 40 doubles and was a very good starting catcher until the end, when Ross took over and became the rock of the team.

Jacoby Ellsbury had an MVP-type season. Jon Lester was tremendous. When Will Middlebrooks had a poor sophomore season, young Xander Bogaerts took over at third base and did a fine job.

Ortiz was a stud. Pedroia had a great year.

Junichi Tazawa and Craig Breslow were dependable out of the bullpen.

Jose Iglesias did a nice job playing all over the infield and then he was used as trade bait to get Peavy, who pitched some big games in the second half.

Cherington never wanted Valentine but Larry Lucchino did, and that's how that went down. After the last-place finish, Cherington gained more power and that's when he made sweeping changes. Those changes started in late August 2012, when he was able to deal Adrian Gonzalez, Carl Crawford, Josh Beckett, and Nick Punto to the Dodgers. That deal led to Cherington needing to bring in a lot of new players for 2013. And, man, did he nail it.

This is a team that won 97 games and went 11–5 in the post-season beating tough opponents—the Rays, Tigers, and then the Cardinals in the World Series.

On August 24, they beat the Dodgers 4–2 and moved into a tie for first. From that point on they went 21–10 and left the competition in the dust. They won the AL East division by six games.

But they were also pretty dominant. In the playoffs they beat aces including Matt Moore, David Price, Justin Verlander, Max Scherzer, Anibal Sanchez, Adam Wainwright, and Michael Wacha.

"I go back to our players understanding their place in this city," Farrell said. "They kind of, for lack of a better way to describe it, they get it. They get that there's, I think, a civic responsibility that we have wearing this uniform, particularly here in Boston. And it became a connection...I'm sure that everybody in our uniform, whether they are here going forward or elsewhere, they'll look back on the events that took place and the way things unfolded as a special year. There's no way we can say it any other way."

The Red Sox had to play a tough opponent in Tampa Bay in the divisional series. I was very impressed with the Rays' pitching throughout the season. But the Red Sox took Game 1, 12–2. Lester gave up a pair of solo homers to Sean Rodriguez and Ben Zobrist before the Red Sox offense bailed him out with a five-run fourth inning when they started hitting doubles, one after another. Lester wound up going 7⅔ innings and allowed only three hits. It was really an excellent outing.

Then in Game 2, the Red Sox touched up David Price for all seven runs in a 7–4 win to take a 2–0 lead. Ortiz hit a couple of home runs, one in the first and the other in the eighth inning. This was too easy. The Rays made it a bit of a challenge, but they knocked into a couple of key double plays to end both the seventh and eighth innings.

Koji, who was such a treat to watch and a fun-loving free spirit, struck out the first two batters he was facing with that 88-mph fastball. Sox fans were all over Wil Myers when he took his position in right field after he'd misplayed a fly ball in Game 1.

Alex Cobb pitched a pretty nice game for the Rays in Game 3 even though the Red Sox got out to a 1–0 lead. The Sox lost it 5–4. The Red Sox actually had a 3–0 lead, but Evan Longoria smashed a three-run homer and Delmon Young drove in the go-ahead run. The Red Sox tied it in the top of the ninth and then we saw something we hadn't seen too often: Koji blowing a game. He had secured the first two outs, but Rays catcher Jose Lobaton blasted a walkoff homer.

The Sox rebounded in Game 4 behind Peavy, who went 5⅔ innings for Boston in what was a scoreless game until David DeJesus doubled in the go-ahead run. The Rays used nine pitchers, which was a postseason record at the time. The Sox scored in the seventh thanks to Ellsbury's legs. We really saw the great ability Ellsbury had. He stole his fourth base of the series and got to third on a wild pitch, which also scored Xander Bogaerts. Shane Victorino legged out an infield hit, which scored another run. And then in the top of the ninth, Fernando Rodney walked two of the first three batters and hit Victorino with two strikes. With the bases loaded, Dustin Pedroia's sacrifice fly added some cushion. Uehara didn't fail this time and got the four-out save. The Sox had made it to the ALCS.

The Tigers were one of those teams that should have won a World Series and it wasn't that Dave Dombrowski, then the Tigers' GM, didn't try. He put together an excellent roster and pitching staff, just as he has with Boston.

Anibal Sanchez, who was the other guy traded with Hanley Ramirez for Mike Lowell and Josh Beckett in 2006, surfaced with the Tigers and struck out 12 batters in a dominant game, beating the Red Sox 1–0. Lester allowed just one run, a Jhonny Peralta RBI single.

In Game 2, Max Scherzer, who has remained one of the top pitchers in the game, held the Red Sox hitless for five innings and Boston trailed 1–0. Clay Buchholz allowed homers to Miguel Cabrera and Alex Avila in the top of the sixth. The Tigers led by five runs. But the Sox came roaring back. Big Papi blasted a two-out grand slam tying the score 5–5.

The highlight reel here was watching Torii Hunter diving over the right-field wall trying to catch Ortiz's drive. Koji stopped Detroit in the ninth in a tie game. Jonny Gomes started the winning rally in the bottom of the ninth with a single. The Tigers then were loose on defense. Rick Porcello tossed a wild pitch that sent Gomes to third, and he scored on Saltalamacchia's walkoff base hit.

Game 3 was such a great game. Justin Verlander allowed a solo homer to Mike Napoli in the seventh inning and that was all the scoring. John Lackey was superb, and the Sox used a threesome of Breslow, Tazawa, and Uehara to finish off the 1–0 shutout. There was an electrical issue in the second inning at Comerica which halted play for 17 minutes.

The Sox had one of those bad games in Game 4 as Peavy was blistered for five runs in the second inning and the Tigers took a 7–3 win.

The Sox took Game 5, 4–3, when Napoli hit a 445-foot blast off Sanchez in the second inning that spearheaded a three-run inning.

The important run came in the third inning when Napoli scored on a wild pitch by Sanchez. Koji again was big at the end in preserving the lead.

In the clinching Game 6, Shane Victorino hit a one-out grand slam against Jose Veras in the seventh that gave Boston a 5–2 lead and the win.

The World Series began and once again the opponent was the St. Louis Cardinals, who had beaten the Pirates and Dodgers to get to the World Series after a 97-win regular season. The Red Sox pummeled them in Game 1, 8–1, behind Lester's 7⅔ shutout innings. A three-run double by Napoli and a two-run homer by Ortiz were the big blasts.

Then in Game 2, the Red Sox suffered their first World Series loss since Game 7 of 1986. The Red Sox actually led 2–1 in this one after Ortiz's two-run homer in the sixth. But a sloppy Sox defense cost them in the seventh. It was a weird play. The bases were loaded. Breslow was pitching to Matt Carpenter, who hit a fly ball to left field. The runner at third beat the throw home but Saltalamacchia botched the throw. The ball was picked up by Breslow, who made a poor throw to third base which allowed Jon Jay to score, giving the Cards a 3–2 lead. Trevor Rosenthal ended it by striking out the side in the ninth.

The Cardinals continued their momentum with a 5–4 win in Game 3. Peavy allowed two runs in the first inning, and while he got better and squirmed out of a bases-loaded, nobody-out situation in the fourth, the Sox weren't able to fully recover. Bogaerts tripled to lead off the fifth inning and scored on a fielder's choice by Mike Carp. Daniel Nava drove in Victorino in the sixth to tie the game. The Cards scored two more but Rosenthal wasn't able to complete a five-out save, with the Sox coming back in the eighth inning with two more runs.

But in the ninth, Koji allowed a first-pitch double to Allen Craig after Yadier Molina had singled. Molina was tagged out at home on a grounder that Pedroia made the play on. Salty threw the ball down to third to see if there was a double-play opportunity but Sox third baseman Will Middlebrooks had the ball get away from him. Craig stumbled over Middlebrooks and umpire Jim Joyce ruled there was obstruction by Middlebrooks and awarded Craig the plate and a walkoff victory.

The loss didn't distract the Red Sox. They bounced right back to beat the Cards 4–2 in Game 4 thanks mostly to Gomes' three-run homer with two outs in the sixth inning. That's what we mean by the flair for the dramatic that Gomes possessed. This one also ended strangely when Koji picked off pinch runner Kolten Wong to end the game.

Game 5 featured a battle of aces, Adam Wainwright vs. Lester. But this one was all Lester, who pitched 7⅔ innings, a real gem. Ortiz knocked in Boston's first run with a double, driving in Pedroia who had also doubled. Matt Holliday tied the game with a solo homer in the fourth, but the Red Sox scored twice when Ross and Ellsbury drove in runs. The Cards got a one-out double by David Freese, but Lester was removed, and Koji came on to record the four-out save.

And we know what happened in Game 6. All Lackey.

It was a pretty special time for Lackey, who had been the whipping boy of Red Sox fans. He was a main character of the 2011 chicken-and-beer team, where pitchers would go into the clubhouse during games and drink beer and eat fried chicken. It was a huge story at the time and a source of great embarrassment to Red Sox management.

But in 2013, Lackey was playing the role of World Series hero. He pitched 6⅔ innings and allowed one run in the clinching Game 6 of the World Series. He became the first pitcher to win World Series clinchers for two franchises. (Lackey won Game 7 for the Angels over the Giants when he was a 24-year-old rookie in 2002.)

The win was also the first World Series Game 6 at Fenway since the Carlton Fisk home run game of 1975. Luis Tiant, the '75 Game 6 starter, tossed the ceremonial first pitch to Fisk.

Ellsbury, who was playing in his last game with the Red Sox before accepting a seven-year, $153 million deal with the Yankees in 2014, singled to right. After Pedroia went out on a grounder to third, Wacha intentionally walked World Series MVP Ortiz (.688). Napoli struck out and then Gomes was hit by a pitch to load the bases.

Victorino, whose walkup song was Bob Marley's "Three Little Birds" ("Every little thing gonna be all right!"), belted a 2-1 pitch off the Covidien sign on the Green Monster, driving in three runs with the double.

In the fourth, Drew led off with a homer into the Red Sox bullpen. Wacha allowed a double to Ellsbury. Wacha, the MVP of the NLCS, was lifted after intentionally walking Ortiz. Napoli made it 5–0 with a single to center off Lance Lynn. After a walk to Gomes, Victorino struck again with a single to left and it was 6–0.

An interesting thing happened in the seventh inning, when with two outs the Cardinals started to rally with a single, a double, and Carlos Beltran's RBI single. Farrell came out to get Lackey, but Lackey told Farrell, "This is my game!" Farrell went along until Lackey walked Matt Holliday to load the bases, at which point Farrell came out again and took his pitcher out.

"I think it might be the most special out of all the World Series that I have been part of, to be honest with you," said Ortiz, who was named MVP. "This is the kind of situation where the unpredictable happens. And this year I think that people predicting third place in the division, maybe last, because of what happened last year. It helped us out. We had a little chip on our shoulder that we want to come in and put up a good run and thank God we did."

Ortiz went 11-for-16 in the Series and reached base in 19 of his 25 plate appearances. He scored seven runs in the six games.

The scoreboard read: 2013 World Champions.

"It was crazy, absolutely crazy," Pedroia said. "It was just an unbelievable feeling to do this in front of our fans. To be honest with you, it was hard to keep the emotions down."

Gomes, who was such a big part of the Boston Strong movement after the bombings, said, "We didn't put Boston on our back.

Koji Uehara and catcher David Ross celebrate after the Red Sox won the 2013 World Series, the team's third championship since 2004. (AP Images)

Boston put us on its back. I don't think a win-loss record sums up how much we care."

Red Sox executive Dr. Charles Steinberg had a great quote afterward. He said, "Sometimes, you recognize baseball history as it's being written. This year, we were recognizing American history as it's being written. For the Red Sox to have the honor of playing a small role in the healing of the city is something that each of these players should really be proud of for the rest of their lives."

Ortiz said, "This is a city that we've been through a lot of situations. Sometimes, bad things got to happen for us to get the message. And we got the message. Everybody stayed together. And it showed the whole world that this is the best of every place."

The reason Ortiz thought this was the most special championship?

"I say this because this is a team that we have a lot of players with heart," said Ortiz. "We probably don't have the talent that we have in '07 and '04. But we have guys that are capable to stay focused and do the little things. And when you win with a ballclub like that, that's special.

"When we started rolling, no one could stop this train."

CHAPTER 9
2018

The Red Sox might have won 108 games, more than any team in baseball, but beating the Yankees in the playoffs, who finished in second place but won 100 games in their own right, wasn't exactly a slam dunk.

The Yankees had a tough, tough lineup. If there was one thing the Red Sox could exploit, it would be New York's starting pitching, and that's what they did. The Red Sox won their first playoff series since 2013 by beating the Yankees in four games to advance to the ALCS against Houston.

The Red Sox won Game 1 at Fenway 5–4 after almost squandering a 5–0 lead. J.D. Martinez had hit a three-run homer. Chris Sale left the game with a 5–0 lead in the sixth inning, outdueling J.A. Happ. Then in Game 2, David Price's postseason woes continued when he was knocked out in the second inning, allowing three runs. Gary Sanchez hit two homers and Aaron Judge also homered in the loss.

But that was the lowest point for Price and the Red Sox even as the ALDS shifted to Yankee Stadium.

Leave it to a Red Sox–Yankees clinching game to end with a review of a groundout! But that's what happened. Craig Kimbrel had a tough time holding a 4–1 lead in the ninth. It was 4–3 when Gleyber Torres grounded to third. Eduardo Nunez charged the weak chopper and his throw just beat Torres, or did it? On the play Nunez hurt himself and the trainer came out to tend to him while the replay challenge occurred. When the review came back in Boston's favor, the celebration ensued.

The Red Sox actually outscored the Yankees 20–4 over the two games at Yankee Stadium, winning Game 3 by a 16–1 score after losing Game 2 at Fenway, which at the time created a little bit of uneasiness for Red Sox fans and the media heading into New York.

It's funny, Alex Cora's moves really stood out in Game 3 because he benched four guys and the ones he replaced them with all came up big. That was the game Brock Holt hit for the cycle. Rafael Devers had replaced Nunez and contributed with a big hit. Nathan Eovaldi pitched seven solid innings and allowed only one run.

After the Yankees beat the Sox 6–2 in Game 2 at Fenway, Judge walked by the Red Sox clubhouse with a speaker that was playing "New York, New York." This was not lost on the Red Sox players who used it as motivation in Game 3. It sounds like they took it really personal considering the 16–1 rout.

Then in Game 4, Rick Porcello pitched well and won his first ever playoff game. And then Cora brought on Chris Sale in relief in the eighth inning before Kimbrel came on for a shaky ninth inning. But the job got done.

"A lot of people gave up on us after Game 2," Cora said. "We showed up last night and tonight and had our plan all mapped out. At the end he wasn't the usual Craig Kimbrel, but he got three outs."

One of the funnier things that happened in that series was reliever Ryan Brasier yelling at Sanchez to get into the batter's box after Sanchez was lingering outside the box and making Brasier wait. It kind of showed the mentality the Red Sox players had in that series.

Of course, with Cora having been the bench coach in Houston when the Astros won their World Series in 2017, there was a lot of talk about what advantages Cora might have over his old team. While everyone tried to downplay it, it turns out he might have had some inside knowledge of their players as the Red Sox went on to win the series in five games, winning it on the road in Houston, a tough place to play.

Maybe the Astros weren't as good as they had been in '17. Jose Altuve didn't have a full year because of injuries, nor did shortstop

Carlos Correa. And the production of some of their other hitters wasn't as great, though third baseman Alex Bregman really emerged as a superstar player.

But as much as this was probably the scariest team they had to face, I still believed the Red Sox would beat the Astros.

It started ominously in Game 1 at Fenway. Sale didn't have his best and struggled with his location in a 7–2 loss. This was a close game, 3–2 Astros, until they broke it open with four runs in the ninth inning.

Of course, a controversy developed after that game as to whether the Astros were spying on the Red Sox. Security noticed a person in the camera well on the third-base side, facing the Red Sox dugout. It turned out to be an Astros employee. MLB investigated and said they were shooting the Sox dugout to make sure they weren't trying to steal signs. The topic was dropped, but the Red Sox weren't too pleased.

The Red Sox got a huge third-inning three-run double by Jackie Bradley Jr. in Game 2 against Gerrit Cole that gave the Red Sox a 5–4 lead. The big thing in this one was 3⅓ hitless and scoreless innings by the Red Sox bullpen, until Kimbrel struggled in the ninth. But they held on to even the series.

Tied up, the teams shifted to Houston for three games. Cora received all kinds of attention from the Houston media upon his return. In a nice matchup of Eovaldi vs. former AL Cy Young winner Dallas Keuchel, Eovaldi was the clear victor with six solid innings, allowing two runs in an 8–2 win in which Steve Pearce hit a solo homer in the sixth inning to give Boston a 3–2 lead they wouldn't relinquish.

More controversy ensued in Game 4. In the first inning, Mookie Betts was interfered with as he leaped for a ball that was heading into the stands, only to have a fan interfere with him. That's the way

Joe West called the Jose Altuve drive that could have changed the complexion of this 8–6 Red Sox win. The interference call cost the Astros two runs. The Astros led 5–4, but the Red Sox attacked the Astros bullpen, took the lead, and won the game.

Betts was sensational in right field. He made a picture-perfect throw to nail Tony Kemp at second base in the eighth inning as Kemp foolishly tried to stretch a single into a double. It proved to be a huge break for the Red Sox, as they warded off an Astros comeback in what had been a back-and-forth game.

And let's not forget the great defensive play by Andrew Benintendi in the ninth inning to rob Alex Bregman and end Game 4 in spectacular fashion. Benintendi ran in hard and took quite a chance when he dove and caught the ball before it hit the grass. He was able to show the ball in his glove to the umpire, who ruled it an out.

So, it wasn't just pitching and hitting, it was great defense.

The Red Sox were really relentless. You could sense that the Astros were on the ropes and ready to go down. As much as they fought in these games, the Red Sox always had an answer. It had to be exhausting.

Then in the clincher, Game 5 in Houston, Cora pulled a switch with his starter. He wanted to give Sale, who had been limited because of his sore shoulder, more time. Cora went to David Price on three days' rest. Price was more than eager to take the ball against his former Tigers teammate, the great Justin Verlander.

He certainly won the Sox fans over with six shutout innings, three hits, nine strikeouts, and no walks. It was vintage Price in a 4–1 clinching win. J.D. Martinez hit a solo shot off Verlander and third baseman Rafael Devers hit a three-run homer in the sixth.

"One of the most special days I've ever had on a baseball field," Price said after the game as he held his infant son in his arms. "It was something special for all of us. To do what we did in New York and then beat the reigning champs…I kept telling myself to stay in the moment. I was able to do that tonight."

Cora was so happy for Price, who had been ridiculed for his poor postseason record, 0–9 in 11 postseason starts before this win.

"What will we do now that we don't have David Price to kick around anymore?" Cora asked.

Astros manager A.J. Hinch was impressed after the loss. He said, "They put pressure on you from the very beginning and they don't let up. And when people doubted them, they just got better."

We opened the World Series at Fenway with an electric crowd that was in on every pitch. There was no getting up to get a beer or a hot dog. The fans were completely in it. The Red Sox were certainly going to take advantage of their home-field advantage. I've always said that the Fenway crowd provides a certain 10th man that you just don't see in too many other places. First off, the ballpark is intimidating to the opposing players and you have the feeling that the fans are right on top of you. I just had a feeling after they took care of the Astros that they'd beat the Dodgers.

I don't know if the Dodgers felt that heat at Fenway but the Red Sox won Game 1 anyway, 8–4. This was a good game. The Dodgers cut the Red Sox lead to 5–4 with shortstop Manny Machado's sacrifice fly in the top of the seventh. But in the bottom of the seventh, Eduardo Nunez belted a three-run homer off lefty Alex Wood that pretty much sealed it. Talk about clutch. Nunez, in my opinion, didn't get enough credit for putting the finishing touches on that win. Since the Red Sox had acquired Nunez in a trade deadline deal in July of 2017, he had produced some big hits and was a very useful player.

Game 2 was a well-pitched game by David Price, who got a couple of great defensive plays from Rafael Devers at third base and

Andrew Benintendi in left field. Devers' play occurred in the sixth, robbing Chris Taylor of a hit. Benintendi made a leaping catch near the left-field scoreboard to rob Brian Dozier in the fifth with the Dodgers up 2–1. The Red Sox broke this open when five straight hitters reached base with two outs in the fifth inning. J.D. Martinez provided the big hit, a two-run single.

Most people had to rewatch Game 3 at Dodgers Stadium two nights after, because it went 18 innings, and who was up? It was like 3:30 in the morning back in Boston when the Red Sox lost a heart-breaking game 3–2 when Max Muncy homered in the bottom of the 18th off Nathan Eovaldi.

This was a like a Rocky–Apollo Creed heavyweight fight. Who would be the last man standing? But while many thought the loss would demoralize the Red Sox, it actually lifted them up. After all, Eovaldi, in defeat, came out of that game as an all-time Red Sox hero. While Alex Cora had to carefully navigate the game with his pitching staff, Eovaldi wound up throwing 97 pitches and pitched six innings in relief in one of the gutsiest performances you'll ever see. Eovaldi had had two Tommy John surgeries, and you wondered whether such a stressful performance would get him hurt, but it turned out to be one of the most inspirational pitching performances you'll ever see.

The game itself was remarkable. The game saw 46 players. There were 561 pitches thrown by 18 pitchers. There were a combined 34 strikeouts, which was a postseason record. It was certainly a must-win situation for the Dodgers, but boy did they have to work to get it. I felt so bad for Eovaldi, who was pitching on short rest and pitched his heart out. Every inning Cora would ask him if he was okay. And when the 18th rolled around, Cora asked Eovaldi once more if he was okay, and Eovaldi said that he wanted to finish off the inning. Well, it didn't work out, but the way he was throwing, hitting 100 mph with that power arm, prior to Muncy going deep, the Dodgers couldn't make any substantial contact.

And the next day, Eovaldi walked into Cora's office and told him that he could pitch that night again if needed.

The Red Sox could have gone one way or the other. They could have folded from fatigue and been down as a team, or they could band together and be inspired by Eovaldi. They chose to be inspired.

But Game 4 didn't start well for the Red Sox. Rich Hill, a native of Milton, Massachusetts, pitched the game of his life. He was up 4–0 in the seventh inning with one out and one on when Dodgers manager Dave Roberts left the dugout. As it turned out there was much confusion about Roberts' visit. Hill thought Roberts was coming to take him out of the game, so he handed the ball to Roberts. But Roberts' version is he wasn't coming to take him out, just to see if his pitcher was okay. Hill had thrown 91 pitches, which he thought meant he was coming out. Roberts made the move to Scott Alexander because he felt that by Hill giving him the ball, it meant he was done.

It's funny that Roberts is the man credited most with the Red Sox winning the 2004 World Series with his incredible steal of second base in Game 4 of the ALCS against the Yankees in 2004 with Boston down 0–3 and on the brink of elimination.

The move to remove Hill proved to be a massive break for the Red Sox. They were now in the Dodgers bullpen, which didn't pitch well in the series. The Red Sox scored eight earned runs off their relievers and pulled off a win that looked so improbable for almost seven innings. Steve Pearce hit one of his three homers in the final two games to lead the assault.

Up 3–1, the Sox came into Game 5 with all of the momentum. The David Price–Clayton Kershaw matchup was quickly slanted toward Price, who redeemed himself in a big way with Red Sox fans. Pearce homered off Kershaw in the first inning after Andrew Benintendi singled to give Boston a quick 2–0 lead. Price went on to allow only three hits over seven innings. Pearce hit a second homer in the eighth inning and won the MVP of the series.

What was amazing was how well the Red Sox played on the road in the postseason; they outscored their opponents 56–23 in the three series. Red Sox owner John Henry declared after the game, "This is the greatest Red Sox team ever!" And it's a statement I can't disagree with. What they did was so impressive, so dominant. After winning 108 regular season games, they went 11–3 in the postseason. They clinched all three playoff series on the road against the Yankees, Astros, and Dodgers.

As my old broadcast partner Ned Martin often said, "Mercy!" To have recovered enough from my cancer treatments to watch it all unfold in the postseason and watch it happen made me one happy man.

CHAPTER 10
MY ALL-TIME FAVORITE PLAYERS

I've been around a lot of players both as a player and broadcaster, but there are players I've covered as a broadcaster who I've thoroughly enjoyed. I've commented a lot about Pedro Martinez, Roger Clemens, and Jason Varitek, so they are on the list, no doubt. Here are some of the others who I came to enjoy as personal favorites, in no particular order.

David Ortiz

The best clutch hitter in Red Sox history. He won championships with his swings. To think, he didn't even have the starting job when he first got to Boston in 2003. Jeremy Giambi was the DH but after a while Ortiz's presence was too much to ignore. For a guy Theo Epstein picked up off the scrap heap, he was a force. He will be a Hall of Famer. He'll go down as one of the greatest Red Sox players ever. He had a profound effect on Red Sox teams as a leader. He'd take a guy aside and let him know what was on his mind. He had the complete respect of his teammates.

Mo Vaughn

I loved watching Mo's power uppercut swing. He hit some mammoth homers. He was another player who had the flair for the dramatic. With that left-handed swing he could hit the ball the other way and therefore was really suited for Fenway Park. He was very smart. He was a very underrated defensive first baseman. It was sad when he left as a free agent and signed with the Angels and then got traded to the Mets. He was a guy who was a fan favorite and should have spent his entire career in Boston.

Dustin Pedroia

I must admit, I blew it with this one. When I first saw him come up I saw this little guy with this big swing and he had a really bad first month. Then, well, he proved the world wrong. He became the second-greatest second baseman in Red Sox history behind Bobby Doerr. He became Rookie of the Year and MVP of the league. He played every play 100 percent. Now we can watch his comeback from the knee surgery he had. I would never bet against him again.

Nomar Garciaparra

Nomar was generally liked and respected by all the fans. My regret for Nomar is I wish he could have enjoyed his time as a player more in Boston. He was a great hitter and had such fast hands. His actions reminded me of Paul Molitor. He didn't care for the media attention in Boston, which I think weighed heavily on him at times. But his talent was something that you never forget.

Wade Boggs

I had the good fortune to not only play with Wade but cover him as well. I remember when he first came up from Pawtucket, we thought, "Okay, there's got to be a way he's going to be pitched and it's going to be tough for him." That never happened. He was a great hitter from Day One. The other thing was his defense. When he first came up he wasn't that good. But I don't think I ever saw a guy work harder on his defense to the point where he became a Gold Glove third baseman. That came with the Yankees, but he was good with the Red Sox as well. It's no surprise he's a first ballot Hall of Famer.

Mike Lowell

What a great guy. He was 100 percent pure genuine. He was an excellent third baseman and he was the MVP of the 2007 World Series. He was a really good hitter. The Red Sox got criticized for trading Hanley Ramirez to the Marlins for Lowell and Josh Beckett. Imagine, Lowell was the "throw-in" in that deal. The Marlins just needed the Red Sox to pick up his contract, which called for $9 million per year in '06 and '07. Mike hit .400 in 15 at-bats in the World Series sweep against the Colorado Rockies. That was after hitting .324 and knocking in 120 runs in the regular season.

Manny Ramirez

Manny was entertaining and probably one of the best right-handed hitters I have ever seen. People thought Manny just went through the motions, but that was hardly the case. He worked very hard at hitting. He was a hitting savant, much like J.D. Martinez. Manny didn't care much about playing left field, but he wasn't horrible out there. His antics would crack us up. The play we still talk about to this day was the one where Johnny Damon was trying to throw to the cutoff man and Manny made a dive for the ball and caught it. It was classic Manny. Things didn't end well for him and eventually he was caught for PEDs. Too bad, because his numbers—555 homers, 1,831 RBIs, and a .996 OPS—certainly warrant his induction into the Hall of Fame.

Curt Schilling

Big-game pitcher. Just look at that postseason record: 11–2, 2.23 ERA. He was the guy you felt most comfortable giving the ball to. What he did to pitch in the "Bloody Sock" game was above and beyond. A couple of things about Curt. I remember being on the air talking about his split-fingered pitch and I actually showed the audience the grip. He must have been watching in the clubhouse, because he called me the next day and said, "If I gripped the ball like you described, it would land over the Green Monster." He proceeded to tell me that the grip was wrong because it needed to be along certain seams of the ball. The other thing he always said was there's no such thing as a waste pitch. Even on 0-2. He said every pitch had a purpose and that's the way he approached it.

Jonathan Papelbon

Nothing bothered him. Nothing. He had the perfect closer mentality, which I think is why he was so successful. Looking back, his personality was similar to Patriots tight end Rob Gronkowski's: loves to have fun and seems to not have a care in the world but also very talented.

Craig Kimbrel

I love his makeup. He has that 97-mph fastball and a breaking ball that makes hitters buckle. I admire him for playing the season knowing his infant daughter was facing multiple heart surgeries. That can't be easy. Kimbrel is one of the best closers in baseball.

Mookie Betts

A five-tool player and really probably the most talented player I've ever been around. Earlier I wrote about Nomar's fast hands. Mookie's hands are even faster. Here's a guy who was a second baseman for most of his life but then his only path to the big leagues was to play right field. Well, it's not that easy, but he managed to become the best outfielder in baseball in a very short time. Power, speed, defense, hitting for average—you name it, he can do it.

He's still not in the prime of his career and he has already won the American League MVP. I'm not sure there's ever been a greater athlete in Boston.

Xander Bogaerts

So smooth. He just glides through the field. Believe me, I'm not comparing him to Joe DiMaggio because that would be unfair, but Joe D. would also glide all over the field. Xander does things with such grace and ease. Fred Lynn was like that. Xander had his breakthrough year in 2018 when, in my opinion, he put together the

Xander Bogaerts and Mookie Betts should be part of the Red Sox's foundation for years to come. (AP Images)

offense, the power we know he has, and his defense was excellent. I feel very comfortable with him as our shortstop.

J.D. Martinez

Like I said, he has similar traits to Manny Ramirez and Jim Rice. He's a great hitter. It's not often you see that combination of pure hitting and power. Manny and Jimmy had that. And certainly J.D. has it. He has lived up to everything he was advertised as before he got here and more. The fact that he helped so many of his teammates, including Mookie, is a tribute to his team-first attitude. He was the primary DH, but he also played very well in the outfield. Nobody is saying he's as good as Andrew Benintendi, Jackie Bradley Jr., and Mookie, but he could play outfield for most teams full time and I know he likes being a complete player.

Jackie Bradley Jr.

One of the nicest people I've ever met, and I don't think I'll ever see anyone who can play center field like he does. I played with Lynn, who was outstanding, but JBJ has something special going on. The balls he gets to are mind-boggling. It's as if he has a GPS in his body and he knows where the ball is going to go. His reads are amazing. He's just outstanding. His catches are a highlight video. Sometimes he defies gravity. I do believe JBJ will become a complete player. He was always a very good minor league hitter. He had a really good season in 2016 when he was named to the All-Star team. I'm so happy he finally won his first Gold Glove in 2018, which has been long overdue.

Tim Wakefield

Tim won 200 games, 186 with the Red Sox, and pitched until he was 45 years old. I can't tell you how much he contributed to the Red Sox team when he joined them in 1995 after Dan Duquette saved him from the scrap heap. He immediately went on an amazing run and you had to scratch your head and wonder how the Pirates could have just released him. He went on a 14–1 run when he first joined the Red Sox on May 27, 1995. He saved the Red Sox rotation. He went on to serve many roles and even became the Red Sox closer in 1999. He was also one of the most charitable players I've ever known. A great person, who so many times in his 17 years with the Red Sox saved the day.

CHAPTER 11
THE MEMORABLE
HIGHS AND LOWS

That September 28, 2011, night at Camden Yards was pretty surreal. The Red Sox were playing the Orioles and they had to win the game or Tampa Bay had to lose its game against the Yankees for Boston to make the playoffs.

It was looking pretty good for us taking a one-run lead into the ninth inning against Baltimore, and then one out away from a 3–2 victory.

But closer Jonathan Papelbon gave up three straight hits and we lost 4–3. It wasn't over as a Rays loss to the Yankees would have backed the Red Sox into the postseason. But that didn't happen either.

Rays third baseman Evan Longoria saw to that. Moments after the Red Sox had lost, Longoria homered in the 12th inning to give the Rays an 8–7 win, erasing a 7-0 deficit.

The Red Sox had led the Rays by nine games on September 4.

How they lost the final game was also shocking because Carl Crawford, who had signed a seven-year, $142 million deal as a free agent, failed to catch a sinking liner off the bat of Robert Andino, sending Nolan Reimold home with the winning run.

"I knew I couldn't dive for it, had to get under it," Crawford said. "I think the ball tipped my glove. I don't think I've ever been part of something like this. It will go down as one of the worst collapses in history."

All of a sudden, you're sitting there stunned. Instead of heading off to the playoffs, you're heading home. We couldn't believe it. Don Orsillo and I were just watching this with our mouths open, saying, "This is actually over?" And then we have to do the postgame wrap up. I think Orsillo and I both looked like we had died.

The team was prepared to play Texas to start the playoffs. But that wasn't to be. So obviously we headed back to the hotel. I ended up flying home the next day, still trying to digest one of the more stunning collapses in Red Sox history.

You just figured this team, given all of its talent, would make the playoffs. It was kind of like coming back from the morgue. Even the next morning I woke up in disbelief that the season was over.

The one thing that sticks out in my mind was the way that Baltimore was celebrating on the field. It was like they had accomplished something—they had beaten the Red Sox in a very big game. They didn't have much of a year that year and we know how much Buck Showalter loves beating the Red Sox. And he was just standing there watching his team celebrate, thinking it was something to build on hopefully for the next year.

The whole month of September was terrible. The Red Sox finished 7–20. Just awful. Along the way you just felt they weren't going to win many games, but I never felt like they were going to miss the playoffs. I thought they had a good enough club to get in there, and if they did, they could do some damage.

This was a team that had very good players. Jacoby Ellsbury hit 32 home runs and knocked in 105 runs. Adrian Gonzalez had a big year in his first season with the Red Sox: 117 RBIs, 27 homers, a .338 average. Kevin Youkilis, Dustin Pedroia, and David Ortiz all had very good seasons. Jon Lester and Josh Beckett were very good in the rotation. Papelbon saved 31 games. There's no reason this team couldn't have gone far.

Baseball's a different animal than the other sports. It's every day, so you figure every day you go out there, you're going to win. And even though the team was slumping, there didn't appear to be any panic that I could see. Maybe Terry Francona was feeling it, I don't know. But it just seemed like the season was rolling on and you were going to turn this thing around and win the amount of games you had to win and get into the playoffs. This was about as low as you could get for me with the exception of losing the one-game playoff game like we did in 1978.

From a broadcaster's perspective, this is the most shock I had ever experienced about a game and a result.

Then on the flip side of that, you had Joe Morgan's Magic, which was really a fun time. It was early in my broadcasting career and those 1988 Red Sox had underachieved for much of the first half of the season, 43–42 at the time John McNamara was fired on July 15.

Morgan won 12 straight and 19 out of 20 to begin his tenure.

Before Lou Gorman, our general manager at the time, gave the job to Joe permanently, we were looking for another manager, and the hot story was that Joe Torre was going to come and manage the Red Sox.

I honestly believe through the first maybe five or six wins that they still had their eye open for another manager. But the team just refused to lose. There was an incredible thing going on. You had guys like Todd Benzinger and Kevin Romine winning games with big hits.

It just kept going on and on and on, and I think finally they got to a point where Lou and Haywood Sullivan, one of the owners, just said, "Wait a minute, we probably don't need another manager. We've got something good going."

It was pretty remarkable because you didn't expect the team to make a run like that. The way they had been playing, where the team seemed a bit listless, to go from that to all of this energy and excitement was one of those rare baseball experiences where you go on the field and everything goes your way. You just don't see that very often.

It wasn't a great team at that point. Obviously when you're looking for a new manager, things can't be that great. But Joe made it great. I don't know if Joe was just a breath of fresh air for the players or the team just coincidentally started to play better.

I've been in a situation as a player when we changed managers back in my Angels days. Dick Williams got fired in my second year in baseball and they named Norm Sherry the manager. I was crushed, because it was Williams who brought me to the big leagues. It was Grover Resinger, Dick's top confidante and coach, who had really held my hand from the day I met him in Triple-A through my rookie season. Grover was my mentor with the Angels, and all of a sudden they were gone. I remember being so pissed at the time that the first game I played under Norm Sherry, I was hustling my butt off because I was so upset. I wanted to prove they had made a mistake. It was a weird feeling. It was an empty feeling because I felt like I lost my security blankets.

I can't say that '88 team responded because of the change of manager, I think things just started to click. And I also think that particular group didn't think that Morgan was going to be there very long. I don't think they figured him to be a permanent manager with all the rumors going around that they were looking for somebody else.

I've never been one to believe that a midseason change like that makes a huge difference. But they were playing their asses off on the field, so Joe should get the credit for that.

I really wasn't surprised McNamara was fired. John had been here quite a while and the shelf life, I've always said about managers in Boston, isn't that long. Expectations are so high, and when the team is underachieving obviously the manager becomes the person you point at.

They can't get rid of the players. They can make changes but they can't overhaul everything. John had his run here, there's no question about that. I think it was time for them to probably make the move, and they did. And "Walpole Joe," as he was called given the town he was from, became the fan favorite.

I really give all the credit to the players on that because you just don't run off streaks like that because you got a new manager. A lot of things have to go right. And I don't mean that disparagingly to Joe, it's just that it's the players who are out there playing and doing the job. It's their responsibility. When I played for a manager who got fired, I always felt like it was our fault because we didn't do a good job. I never played for a manager who I disliked and I hoped got fired.

You're concerned about your own game. You're concerned about how you're playing, and you've got to continue to play well to be in the big leagues. I never had that experience where I said, "Gee, I hope they fire this guy because I'd play better for someone else."

Of course, the other shocking game was Game 7 of the 2003 American League Championship Series against the Yankees.

Because it was a playoff game, I wasn't broadcasting that one, but like everyone else, I was watching on TV. Before long, my wife, Phoebe, was yelling at the TV. The prevailing theme was that Grady Little left Pedro Martinez in the game too long.

My feeling was Pedro had something left even though he had allowed hits to Derek Jeter and Bernie Williams, making it a 5–3 game. Grady came out to the mound and after talking to Pedro decided to leave him in. Hideki Matsui also got a hit. Then Jorge Posada hit a blooper to center which fell in to tie the game.

I think Grady took a lot of heat. I could understand it from a fan's point of view. From a baseball point of view, I wasn't that against leaving him in. The only problem I had was that I think *Pedro* thought he was coming out. And once a player or a pitcher, in particular, thinks that he's coming out of the game, it's a whole different mindset after that.

I had to listen to my wife yell at the TV at Grady, which all of New England was doing.

I wasn't as angry as everybody else in the baseball world was. I figured you've got Pedro Martinez out there, leave him out there. Of course, at that time the bullpen was lights out, too. And I think the combination of having a good bullpen and Pedro maybe looking like he was tiring is what made people mad.

That '03 team was an outstanding offensive team. It was really the start of the Golden Era of Red Sox baseball. For the first time in a while, people thought they could beat those great Yankees teams.

That team led the league in just about every offensive category. They scored 961 runs. They hit .289. They had an on-base percentage of .360 and slugged at .491, which was even higher than the 1927 Yankees.

It was the year that the Red Sox introduced David Ortiz into the lineup at DH. They started the year with Jeremy Giambi, but when he slumped Big Papi got his chance and he didn't disappoint.

It was just a great lineup with a great hitting approach. Bill Mueller, who was one of my favorite guys on the team, won the batting title with a .326 average. They had Johnny Damon, Todd Walker, Trot Nixon, Manny Ramirez, Jason Varitek, and Nomar Garciaparra. Just a stacked lineup. Ron "Papa Jack" Jackson was the hitting coach and he did a great job with the hitters.

They beat the Oakland A's in the divisional series in five games after being down 2–0. And then, in Game 3 of the ALCS against the Yankees, there were more fireworks. In a Pedro vs. Clemens pitching matchup, Pedro drilled Karim Garcia in the back and the two exchanged words. Pedro also made a gesture toward Yankees catcher Jorge Posada.

Then Roger threw one high and tight to Manny and he charged the mound, which emptied both benches. It started to look like the old days when I played with the Red Sox and we and the Yankees truly hated one another.

It was surprising to me to see Don Zimmer charge Pedro in front of the Red Sox dugout. Pedro turned and saw him and just tossed him to the ground. Zim was 72 years old at the time. He was my former manager with the Red Sox and I just thought it was a strange sight to see that happen.

Anyway, the Red Sox were ahead in Game 7, 5–2. A three-run lead with Pedro pitching, well, you have to feel good about that. But the Yankees tied it up with three runs in the eighth inning. It went into extra innings and that's when Aaron Boone hit the big first-pitch walkoff home run in the bottom of the 11th against Tim Wakefield at 12:16 AM. The Yankees took the 6–5 win and went on to face Florida in the World Series.

That home run set Yankee Stadium on fire. The fans were absolutely crazy, and it vaulted Boone into Yankees immortality. Now he's their manager.

It was crushing, really, and after that horrible loss, Grady was fired. Terry Francona was brought in. The Red Sox made some additions for '04, including signing Curt Schilling, and the interest in that team just seemed to increase rather than decrease. The feeling was there was a chance to break the 86-year Curse of the Bambino. While people were crushed they didn't do it in 2003, they had hope for 2004.

It's unfortunate that Grady was placed in the same category as Bill Buckner, as something of a villain. It's really awful. I've never been in those shoes where I've had to manage a game and make those kinds of decisions, so it's hard for me personally to go through a manager's thinking, the moves that he has to make or not make. In this case, I was sitting there saying to myself, "Leave Pedro alone. I'd leave him alone. I'm going with my best."

I had a good relationship with Grady, as I did with just about every manager I covered as a broadcaster.

Grady Little takes the ball from Pedro Martinez in Game 7 of the 2003 ALCS against the Yankees. (AP Images)

I'd say the closest relationship I had was with Jimy Williams. Jimy came from the Angels organization and he was always managing a step or two down from where I was playing. So, we kind of had that Angels connection.

I liked Jimy a lot. He was old school, and I think I probably had more baseball conversations with him than anybody else. I remember one night in Montreal back in mid-July of 2001. We were up there playing, and we later went out to dinner. He was as low as low could get, and this was toward the end for him.

On the way back to the car he said, "Rem, I don't think I can do this anymore." The GM was Dan Duquette at the time and Jimy said, "The guy is driving me crazy. I just don't think I can do this anymore."

I felt like I was riding back from dinner with a beaten manager. I knew that when he started telling me stuff that the end was near. I felt bad for him. But it was a perfect example of the incredible pressure that managers, especially those who manage the Red Sox, are under.

If you can crack a guy like Jimy Williams, that's saying a lot because he's a pretty tough guy. He'd been through a lot in his career and finally got the chance to manage the Red Sox. He took a beating when he first came in. I remember his first press conference in November of 1997 where everybody was making fun of him because of the way he talked and the things that he said.

He was known for his funny quotes like, "If a frog had wings, it wouldn't bump its booty." But he was a first-class individual.

I've had good relationships with all of the Red Sox managers. John Farrell was great, and we had cancer in common. We talked a lot about that. When I'm dealing with a manager I try to ask questions that are relevant to the game. I don't try to take up a lot of their time because their time is precious. You know how busy they are, what they've got to deal with media-wise, player-wise, preparation-wise, so I'm not one to go in and sit there and bullshit for a half hour. There are times I ask a question just for my own understanding and not something I'm going to repeat on the air. I think they respect me and trust me for that. So, I get information that you normally probably wouldn't get. I try to stay away from trying to find out a lot of inside stuff. If they want to talk, I let them talk and I listen. Once in a while I'll give an opinion, but I do my best to not be the type of guy who goes into the manager's office, sitting there unannounced.

Kevin Kennedy was a little bit different. He and Duquette didn't get along at all and frequently were at odds, even though Dan brought Kevin here from their Montreal days together. I was shocked how their relationship deteriorated during the time that he was the manager here.

I wasn't as close to Kevin as the others. I can't say that he was bad to me at all. But he had a very large ego which alienated him from players and others as well.

I always got along great with Duquette. He was great to me. Of all the general managers that I've been around, he was terrific with me. And he still is.

I kind of felt bad for him when the Red Sox won in 2004 because, nothing against Theo Epstein, but a lot of that team was put together by Duquette. We were at the World Series game and he had seats very close to where I was sitting on the third-base side near the dugout. It was shocking to me. Here's the guy who really put this team together with the exception of a few players, and he's literally sitting in the stands. It was a weird feeling to see that.

"Duke" would talk to you a bit. A lot of the others were very quiet. Ben Cherington was very quiet. Theo was quiet. It's not like the old days when the general managers used to float around and bullshit with the press, go have a pop with them after the game and stuff like that. Times have certainly changed. It's not like that anymore.

Lou Gorman was a great talker. He was an old-school guy. He talked a lot about baseball, but he was funny. He was a great human being, he really was. You could feel very comfortable going up and talking baseball with him and he'd probably say things he shouldn't say.

Even now, Dave Dombrowski is a bit more of an old-school general manager, even though he's the president of baseball operations. But you ask him a question, he'll give you an honest answer. I've never been around a general manager who travels with the club as much as he does. Never. He's on 95 percent of the trips. That's hard to do, but he feels like he wants to be close to the ballclub, to get the feel of the club. When I played, it used to be a big deal if a general manager made a trip. We'd say, "Oh shit, we gotta be on our toes."

Also, I can honestly say that I've really never had a beef with a player in all my years in broadcasting. I know that things we say on TV get back to the players. Or they sit in the clubhouse and wonder what the hell we're talking about. I know that. But what I've always done as part of my job is make myself accessible to the players. I get to the clubhouse at a time when they're very relaxed, before the regular media gets in there.

The older I get, the worse I'm getting as far as how early I get to the ballpark. I'm in there some days at 1:30 PM for a 7:00 PM game. I beat a lot of the players to the ballpark. If the managers get there early, I like to get there early. I enjoy that time very much, sitting around and talking a little bit.

I don't go up and sit near the players' lockers and bullshit with them because I remember not liking that when I was a player. I wanted to be by myself, I wanted to be with my own thoughts, I wanted to be with my teammates and talk to them. I don't want to be a pain in their ass, but I also want to be available, so if anybody has a beef with anything that maybe I've said, I'm there. I'm accountable.

That's not to say they don't think I've made mistakes on TV. One thing I am willing to do is if I say something wrong, I try to correct it. Any analyst who tells you that everything they say is correct is full of it. A lot of analysts act like what they say is gospel. Well, that's not true. You make mistakes as an analyst. So if a player has an issue with something you may have said or how you said it, I'm there to listen. And if they're correct and I'm wrong, I'll go on the air and I'll correct it. I've done that in the past. I think I get a little respect because of that. I think if they don't see the broadcasters around and they're making comments in the booth, I don't think they respect that. That's the way I've always tried to do it.

When I got the job, originally, I was down there with the guys who I played with. I kind of kept that style, and I liked it. And it's not like I'm getting inside information. I'm not getting anything different than the rest of the media gets. I just enjoy being in the atmosphere, and it's like I'm getting ready to play a game. It makes me feel like I'm still a little bit of a player.

I've seen a lot of different types of players in my career as a player and a broadcaster. There are the very serious ones. There are the ones who like stay loose. There are ones who are in between. And then there are the ones you can't forget because they're a little bit off center.

Jonathan Papelbon was one of the strangest and craziest I've ever been around. He was always doing something crazy, but he was great. He had a great personality. I remember one time he was walking out to the bullpen and we had a camera set up out there and there was a microphone near the camera, and all of a sudden, he started to talk to us on TV.

That was Papelbon. Nobody else would ever do that except Pap. He was a character.

There was one issue that popped up one time with Josh Beckett. We were on the plane and he came up to me and said, "Boy, Lester's really pissed at you." I think Jon had pitched that night, and I was curious as to why he would have been pissed. I didn't recall saying anything about him that would get him angry.

I got up right away and I walked back with Beckett and I went up to Jon, who was sitting way, way in the back in the last row. I said, "Jon, Josh tells me you got a problem? Would you like to talk it out?"

He said, "What do you mean I got a problem?" So, Beckett was just busting my balls.

You never know when something like that's going to happen. You're dealing with 25 guys and somebody's probably got a problem with you. I always felt like the best way is to try to sit down with the person, discuss what the problem is. If he's right, I'll admit that I'm wrong. If I feel strongly that I'm correct, I'll tell him off. But I haven't had many of those confrontations.

Even David Price started to come around. When he first came here, he was very quiet. It was tough to get a hello out of him. It was virtually impossible to have a conversation with him, but that was fine with me. If that's his style, more power to him.

There was one point a couple years ago, when I was getting nothing from him, not a hello, not a good-bye, totally nothing. He was going through tough times with his elbow and whatever injury was bothering him and he wasn't in the best of moods. He was miserable. I understood that because when you can't play, you're miserable.

I went up to him and I said, "David, can I sit down with you for five minutes?"

And he said, "No, I'm busy right now."

So I said, "Okay, that's good enough for me. If you don't want to talk that's fine." And I walked away.

I came in the clubhouse a couple weeks later and he couldn't have been nicer. He came up to me and he shook my hand at a time when I had just gotten out of the hospital. He was a totally different person. He asked me how I was feeling and all that stuff, and since that day, we've been great. Every single day he'll say hi to me, even on days he pitches.

You don't know what players are going through. That's part of the deal. You've got to respect how they're feeling and things they're dealing with. You don't know if there's an issue on the field or at home. You don't know what makes guys tick or why they're in certain moods on certain days. If a guy tells me he doesn't want to talk, that's fine. It doesn't bother me. It's just that I'd like to know if I've done something that's wrong. I want to know that.

But in terms of wacky, nobody was crazier than Manny Ramirez. It was mostly fun-loving stuff, but it did turn ugly when he attacked our traveling secretary Jack McCormick in the clubhouse when Jack couldn't accommodate a last-minute order of several tickets for the game that night. Players come in early in the afternoon and give Jack their ticket orders for the game. He is usually able to accommodate everybody except when the order is late and there are more tickets ordered than allotted per player. That was the scenario that night. Jack told Manny politely that he couldn't accommodate the late order. Manny got mad and he took a swing at Jack. It was completely uncalled for. And that was one of the incidents that got Manny traded to the Dodgers in late July of 2008.

Manny, of course, had a great two months with the Dodgers and led them to the playoffs. That's not surprising because Manny was one of the greatest hitters of his generation. He could hit for average and power. He knew how to manipulate the bat. He was a hitting clinic, really. He's a hitter all youngsters should watch because he did it right. And it was rare that Manny would have rage like he did that day with Jack. He was usually a happy-go-lucky guy who often acted and reacted like a child.

He also worked harder than anyone on the team, which was a side of Manny that a lot of fans didn't see. And because he was pretty much not participating with the media, nobody really got to know him. I know he confided in David Ortiz and Pedro Martinez. I know Johnny Damon was able to get to him. But for the most part, Manny stayed to himself.

Damon was another funny guy. He was an outstanding player on the field. He could run and play the outfield well. He was a clutch hitter who showed power from the leadoff spot. One thing he couldn't do well was throw, but that didn't come into play too often.

He was a team leader. Johnny talked to the media almost every night and he took the pressure off of his teammates. He would discuss the game every night with the press whether he did anything significant or not.

He and Kevin Millar also kept things loose in the clubhouse on those 2003 and 2004 teams. He admitted that before some games he and Millar would do shots of Jack Daniel's.

"What we had was one small Gatorade cup with a little Jack Daniel's in it," Millar told ESPN.com. "We passed it around and everyone symbolically drank out of the same cup because we are a team."

That's why I've often said the 2004 team was my favorite.

CHAPTER 12
MY BROADCAST PARTNERS

etting into TV was totally by accident. I was released by the Red Sox in April of 1986 when my knees could no longer hold up. I had 11 operations on my left knee, and back then we just didn't have the advanced orthopedic procedures that we have today, ones that might have saved my career or at least extended it for a couple of years. I had one year left on my contract, so the team and I sat down and tried to figure out what I could for the $485,000 I had left on my deal. I decided to go to work as a coach at Double-A New Britain. I only did the games where they were home. I was getting my feet wet as a coach. The following year, I had interest in managing. I was looking to get the Pawtucket job because it was closer to home. I felt as though I was capable of doing the job. But I never had that opportunity. They had Ed Nottle as their manager and they decided to stay with him. So I decided to take the year off. That was 1987, the year after the Red Sox went to the World Series. That was incredibly tough for me because I had played with some of those guys. Not to be a part of it was tough on me.

While I was off for the year, my agent, Jerry Kapstein, had talked to Claiborne about the possibility of broadcasting, and that's how I got the interview set up. I had multiple interviews but honestly broadcasting was never on my radar screen. I always thought I was going to be a coach or a manager as time went on. It actually ended up being the best thing that ever happened for me because had I gone on to coach or manage, I'd have been fired nine times by now.

To get the broadcasting job with the Red Sox was pretty incredible...until I started it. I hated it because I didn't know what I was doing. I'll never forget our first game. It was in Winter Haven, Florida, in spring training of 1988, and we had a damn rain delay right at the beginning. I was so nervous. We had Joe Giulotti of the *Boston Herald* come in for an interview and Ned basically did the whole interview. I remember the next day, Jim Baker, who was writing for the *Herald* at the time as the TV critic, just ripped me after the game saying, "They'd been better off hiring Joe Giulotti than Remy." So, I was off to a rough start. In those days, they used to have the TV writers, Baker and Jack Craig of the *Boston Globe*, write twice a week. So I used to dread getting up in the morning and picking up the newspapers on those days and seeing how bad I was going to get roasted.

They were right—I was absolutely not good at all. I couldn't get my baseball knowledge across because I just didn't understand TV. Once that started to mix, once I got comfortable with people talking into your earpiece, replays, how to represent the replay, how to anticipate what might happen next, I got better. But that took a long time. I honestly thought about quitting after the year because I thought this wasn't for me. I wanted to go back to try and get a job coaching. But my wife, Phoebe, convinced me to give it a little bit more time to see what happens, so I gave it another year. Even after the second year, I didn't feel really comfortable. But I started to see some improvement and so did the people I worked with.

We just kept at it. Back then, there were not tapes being played for me, there were no simulator games, there was nothing. It was just go on the air and figure it out. I didn't think it would be that difficult and then all of a sudden we were live and I was like, holy shit, I don't know what I'm doing. I didn't know how many outs there were, I didn't know what the score was. It was horrible. It was not a pleasant first couple of years. But then, like I said, when I got used to how TV works, that's when I got more comfortable bringing out baseball and the knowledge that I had from the game which was very clear in my head because I had just finished playing.

It wouldn't have surprised me if they had fired me. I probably wouldn't have cared because I wasn't in love with what I was doing. I

was always kind of a perfectionist and when you're not good at something, you don't feel good about doing it. Fortunately, in those days
we were only doing 81 games, because the other half was on Channel
38 with Sean McDonough and Bob Montgomery.

Ned Martin

I needed a lot of help when I first got into the broadcasting business. I had no idea what I was doing, and I needed someone to hold
my hand for a while and teach me everything.

That man was Ned Martin.

I remember getting interviewed by him when I came over to the
Red Sox after being traded from the Angels on December 8, 1977. It
was a big a thrill for me to be on Red Sox Radio with Ned Martin.

What can I say? Ned was great. He was the perfect guy for me
to get into this business with because I had no experience. He was so
laid-back. He was really a radio guy who was forced into TV. But he
was in on the discussions about who NESN and the Red Sox were
going to hire next and it looked like it came down to Mike Andrews
and me. I think what helped me was the fact that I was current, and
I was from New England. The drawback was that I had absolutely
no TV experience. Apparently, it didn't seem to bother them or
Ned. Mike was a great guy. He was another former Red Sox second
baseman who played on that great 1967 team. The fact Mike didn't
get the job was not a deterrent for his career. Things turned out
great for him as he became the executive director of the Jimmy Fund
and helped raise millions of dollars for kids with cancer. So, you can
understand the high regard I hold him in, given my situation.

Ned broadcast Red Sox on radio and TV from 1961 to 1992. His
voice was so soothing. He just had the perfect pipes to be a baseball
announcer. He had the amazing ability to tell the story of the game.

He reminded me of Dodgers great Vin Scully in that way. And I'm breaking in with a guy like that? I was like the opposite. Maybe that's why we hit it off.

I remember we had a meeting with NESN's Bob Whitelaw, who was doing the hiring at the time. It was myself, Ned, Whitelaw, and John Claiborne, who was in charge of NESN. The interview seemed to go well, and I don't know how much input Ned had, but I got the job. It was great to be with a guy like him because nothing rattled him. The one thing he'd get on me about was butchering the English language, partly because he was so eloquent. I'd get this kick in the leg under the table. Half the time, I didn't know what the heck he was doing. I didn't know what I had said to deserve it, but it must have been some phrase I had used incorrectly. But we got along great. He let me learn on my own and learn from my own mistakes, of which there were plenty. I didn't understand TV, but I understood baseball. At first, I couldn't match the two together. That took time, probably a couple of years.

Ned and I traveled together a lot. But I always seemed to lose Ned at the airport. He'd have a couple of pops and we'd go out to dinner, and then when it was time to get to the gate I can't find Ned, he's walking to the wrong gate. He was a character but I loved him. He was so good to me when he could've been rough on me. Had I broken in with someone else, it would've been impossible. But he was so patient and so good that it helped me stay in the game. I think it would've ended differently had it been somebody else.

It got a little bit difficult the last couple of seasons, as he was aging a little bit and he was getting ready to put it away. But he made some amazing calls in his time in Boston. He covered Carl Yastrzemski's entire Hall of Fame career. He called Yaz's 3,000[th] hit. He called Carlton Fisk's homer in Game 6 of the 1975 World Series. He called Roger Clemens' first 20-strikeout game against Seattle on

April 29, 1986. And he did everything with such flair and class. I couldn't think of anybody better to learn on the job with.

Bob Kurtz

Bob was one of the nicest guys that I've ever met in my life. He didn't have a mean bone in him. He had been our in-studio host for the pre- and postgame shows for a few years, but he was given the unenviable task of replacing the great Ned Martin. Bob did that in 1992 and stayed around until 2000.

He was a very talented announcer in many different ways, in baseball and also in hockey. We had a terrific relationship. He was one of those guys who would rush to everything. Like you get into the game and then he'd rub his hands together and say, "Okay, let's get this over with," like he couldn't wait for everything to pop up. He was good. He didn't last a long, long time because he got an opportunity to go back to Minnesota Wild hockey radio broadcasts. I think his wife also wanted to go back there.

By that time, I felt more comfortable about myself in the booth. He'd have been another great guy to break in with because he was that type of personality. But the time Bob got here, I felt like I was on track of being decent and I had put all the pieces together TV-wise and baseball-wise. I think my broadcasting had improved quite a bit. I guess there was a comfort level that we had between us that I think was very productive and very positive.

Sean McDonough

So then came McDonough, the absolute perfect match for me at that time in my career. The guy is absolutely brilliant, with a photographic memory. He would come in and look at the notes and read them one time and put them aside. Then he would be able to rattle stuff off word for word. It was incredible. I've never seen anything like it in my life. What he did for me was challenge me and bring out my personality.

He knew the game because he spent time broadcasting in the minor leagues with the Triple-A Syracuse Chiefs, which was an affiliate of the Toronto Blue Jays. When you're in the minor leagues, you're always around the coaches, the manager, it's a very small community. The announcers who come from the minor leagues really have a tendency to know quite a bit about baseball because they spend time around those people.

He challenged you very quickly. If you didn't agree with something he said, he'd let you know, and you could have a legitimate discussion about it. He realized I had a dry sense of humor. He brought that out of me. He gave me the popular "RemDawg" nickname. It was the first nickname I'd had since being called "Scoot" as a player. He kept calling me that and it stuck. Soon everyone would call me "RemDawg." I really enjoyed working with him. He was pretty special.

I think it really hurt him when he and the Red Sox parted ways, because his dream had always been to do Red Sox baseball. He was crushed by it. I was crushed by it, because I lost an incredible broadcast partner.

To show you how bright he was—I'm an avid watcher of the soap opera *Days of Our Lives*. So one day the actress Kristian Alfonso, who's from Easton, was at the ballpark. I couldn't believe it. I said, "Look, there's Hope Brady from *Days of Our Lives*." Sean knew nothing about it. So, I started to explain to him what her role on the show was and how at that particular time there was a villain coming after her. Then the camera crew found a guy who looked like a villain in the bleachers.

Sean went back and forth with me and it was almost like he'd been watching it his whole life. I couldn't believe the stuff he was coming up with. We finally got her on camera in the booth after we asked her if she'd come on with us and she was more than gracious. We told her I watched the show and we talked about it for a few minutes. By the time it was over, it's like Sean had been watching it for 30 years. It was amazing to me how he could do stuff like that. So yeah, I can't say enough about him. He was so smart.

I've been able to stay in touch with him and we've run into each other once in a while. I text him every now and then and call him. We don't overdo it. When I get sick, he is always sending me messages, wishing me well and praying for me. It makes you feel good that somebody you have worked with really cares about you. But he's like that, so it comes as no surprise. He's gone on to a great national career. He's one of the youngest to call a World Series game. The Joe Carter call in the 1993 World Series is a classic. But that's Sean. Everything he does, he does it top-notch. It just comes so naturally to him. He was born to do it.

Don Orsillo

One of the biggest problems for Don at the beginning is that he was being compared to Sean, and I thought he did sound a lot like him. But they were two totally different personalities. Don was the worrywart. He was bothered by the McDonough comparisons. I kept trying to tell him, "Don't worry about it, it takes time." Change anywhere takes time but especially so in Boston.

I'll tell you the truth, I feel partially responsible for getting him the job. They filled in with Bob Rodgers, who had done our pregame shows. Don came up to the booth one day and he asked, "Is this job available next year?" I told him I didn't know. I'd never met him before because he was in Pawtucket doing the games on TV and radio there. I remember him sitting right on the steps, right near where I sit in the booth. I kept that in the back of my mind and I went to management and I said, "I see this kid from Pawtucket who has tremendous interest in the job. Maybe you can give him a listen before the season is over."

They did, and they liked what they heard. They liked him so much they hired him. And I'm so happy they did. He was an absolute joy to work with. We clicked so well. It took us I would say two or three years to get real comfortable with each other. We came to find out that we had similar personalities and we liked the same type of humor. We were similar in many, many ways. We went through a lot of off-field life problems together. We became very good friends. When you work with somebody for 15 years, you're going to become close.

The game was obviously the No. 1 priority. But when the games were out of hand and something funny happened, we kind of picked up on it. Now, some people hated that, but some people loved it. That was the type of personalities we had. It's amazing when you go to a baseball game, there's so much downtime that things happen in the stands that all of a sudden are funny. We had a good time laughing. As I said, maybe it wasn't everyone's cup of tea but I think a lot of people really enjoyed that.

Two things that I'll never forget about Don. We did a pizza throw skit that just went on and on. And it was one of the funniest things we ever did. This poor guy was going after a foul ball near the left-field corner on April 16, 2007, and he went for the ball and spilled beer all over himself. But there was a guy a few seats down who threw a slice of pizza at him. We just found this really funny and we went on and on about it and we couldn't stop laughing. But the funniest one was when I lost my tooth during a broadcast on

July 2, 2014. I was just talking, and I lost my tooth. Don comes out with pliers and hammers and screwdrivers and stuff like that. I thought that was pretty funny. Also, one time I embarrassed him because he used to carry this bag with him that had all kind of stuff in it. He had everything in there. I made him unpack his bag on TV and people thought it was hilarious. He had everything from Band-Aids to work stuff to cosmetics, combs, all kinds of crap.

We created a bond after working together for so long. It was very difficult the day we found out that he was leaving. When you're with somebody for so long, it's like a marriage and it's hard when it breaks up. But in this business, you've got to adapt and you kind of move on quickly. It took him no time at all to get a new job. I never thought he would have a problem. People ask me if I tried to save his job, but the answer is that was way beyond my control. I was kind of in shock, like most people were. But no, I never went to anyone about that because I didn't feel it was my position to do so. They had already made a decision and I just didn't feel it was the right thing for me to get involved in. I think he understands that. So now he thrives in San Diego. I saw one poll over there that said he and Mark Grant have an 87 percent popular rating, so that's a good thing.

Dave O'Brien

Dave and I did our first game in spring training and we both felt very comfortable with each other right out of the gate. I think that's important. When you look at O'Brien, he's done so many sports. He's done soccer, basketball, football, and of course baseball. He's done major events. He's a guy who is used to working with a lot of analysts in a lot of different sports. I always feel that the play-by-play guy is the professional in the booth and that I am the amateur.

I knew that I was getting a professional broadcaster. I didn't feel the transition was going to be all that difficult. Quite frankly, it was pretty smooth right from the beginning.

Everyone I've worked with has had a different style and personality. I feel it's my responsibility to adjust to them because as I said, they're the professionals in the booth. So whatever style they have, I feel like it is my responsibility to adjust to them. That's not taking pressure off myself, that's just saying that's my job. These guys went to school for this, they're professional broadcasters. I'm an ex-baseball player. So I just feel like whichever guy was in there, from Ned to Dave, I've had to adjust to their style. Actually, you can take Ned out because I didn't have a clue of what I was doing. But from Kurtz on, I had to really adjust to whatever their style was.

I will say this about Dave and this is the truth: he's probably the most prepared guy that I've ever worked with going into a game. He spends a couple of hours in the booth prior to each game preparing for it. He has little anecdotes on every player. His scorecards are unbelievable to look at because there's so much info written on it. I'll say that from everybody I've worked with, his preparation is second to none. It's been tough on Dave because I've been in and out of the booth because of my illnesses, so he's had to adjust to different color analysts. Hopefully I'll get back in there in 2019 and do about 90 games with him and that will make it easier on both of us. I guess it's normal that the more you work together, the more comfortable you are with each other. I am looking forward to working with him for many years to come.

Dave has been so supportive of me during my health issues. He's checked in on me regularly and always has asked if there was anything he could do for me and that he awaits my quick return from the latest setback. He's been great.

The Crew

The major part of a successful broadcast, in my opinion, are the people who work behind the scenes who never get the credit that the people in front of the microphones get. But without these people there would be no show.

We're very fortunate in Boston to have a tremendous group, both present and past. I have incredible respect for the job that they do. I think one of the things that people don't know are the hours that they put into every broadcast, and how many times a crisis happens in the satellite truck and how quickly they get things fixed. We always seem to get on the air even under the toughest conditions.

Sometimes we get into a town at 4:30 in the morning and the crew has to get there by 10:00 in the morning to set up. A lot of times they've done games with a minimum of two or three hours sleep before going to set up the truck for a series. They're really important to me and I feel like we've got about the best group you could possibly have.

Leading off among this group is Mike Narracci, who is our director. Mike and I have been together for so long now we're like a second baseman and shortstop playing together. He seems to know where I'm going to go with certain things, certain replays. He's the veteran in the truck as far as directing goes, and of all the people who I have to work with from the truck, I think he and I have to be in sync probably more than anyone else. To get the right shot, to get the right call on a play or describing something that may be happening, he's thinking along the same lines as I am. I have tremendous respect for him and we've been good friends for many years.

Jeff Mitchell is our producer. He's a guy who's been around a long, long time; he used to do Mets games with Ralph Kiner and Tim McCarver. They brought him in here a couple of years ago as a veteran guy to lead some younger people in the truck and try to teach them the right way of doing things. While he's our producer, he also sometimes directs. He's responsible for running the show from the open until the close of the game. He's a guy who has seen just about everything in baseball and TV. He's a good teacher for the younger group.

One thing I've respected about NESN is that they've always developed young talent in the trucks and expose them to veteran guys like Narracci and Mitchell, and they develop a whole new set of professionals. One of them is Dan Aspen, who performs both pro-ducing and directing. He's going to be a star. There's no question about that. He's very young but he's very attentive. He's inquisitive. He wants to know about baseball. He wants to learn about it and he's a guy with a bright, bright future.

What I've come to find is that the talented young people behind the scenes often get so much experience and get so good at what they do that they move on to bigger positions. They constantly get offered big roles at other networks and many of them end up leaving. A lot of time frustration sets in with some of the younger people, because they feel they could be doing more. I understand their frustration but also understand that they're getting tremendous experience that will serve them well as they move on to bigger things. I can see that Dan Aspen has grown over the years. He's a true pro and I'm proud to work with him.

Another talented person we have in the truck is Amy Johnson, who is absolutely terrific. She's also in the same position as Dan, where she's doing some producing. She just loads me with informa-tion before and during the broadcast. She's right on top of things all the time. When an important stat comes up in a game or a stat from maybe a year ago or two years ago, she's right in my ear with it. I have that information available. She pays attention to detail and, more importantly, what's going on in the game. She's another rising star at NESN.

Another tremendous talent is Steve Garabedian, a long-time employee at NESN in different roles, who joined our broadcast team this year. I call them "our" team because we are a team. With any of these pieces missing, you don't have the same broadcast. You get so used to being with these people that they're not only coworkers, they're friends.

The time we spend together on planes and the time we spend together before games and after games, it's like a small little family that's a traveling road show. Steve is always up in the booth prior to the ballgame making sure everything's okay with us. He's feeding us our copy for reads, which we have a load of at NESN, and that takes up an awful lot of time. His role is very important, because the promotions, ads, etc., are very important to the bottom line.

Those mentioned are really our premier group that travels and does most of the games. They try to split up some of the producing and some of the directing to try to give everyone flexibility in the truck.

But I need to mention our audio guy, who is so important. People don't think about audio but it's different for every single analyst or play-by-play guy. Everyone likes their audio different and Peter Grenier is a master at knowing what you like. I absolutely drive him crazy because I'm someone who likes my audio very loud. I love a lot of crowd sound because it makes me feel like I'm part of the crowd. He gets the sound level exactly where I want it. A lot of times we don't even have to do a pretest because I know it's going to be right on target once the game starts.

The other thing I love about him is that he's a big Beatles fan. He plays guitar in a rock band on the side. One day we were killing some time up in the booth before the game and he brought his guitar in and we were trying to tape a version of "Norwegian Wood (This Bird Has Flown)" and he actually did a very good job on the guitar. I didn't do so well on the vocals so it never made air but that's one thing that we have in common. He does all kinds of other audio work for the Celtics and Bruins as well. He's working all the time. He's certainly one of my favorites.

Guys from the past who have really helped me but are no longer with NESN are people quite frankly I'll never forget. Russ Kenn was a producer in the Sean McDonough and Don Orsillo era. He was so level-headed and calm. One thing you don't like when you're doing a game is a lot of screaming and yelling coming out of the truck, and he was a guy that got his point across very well but in a low tone. It meant something when he said something. You got exactly what he was talking about and when he had a beef he'd let you know but in a pleasant way. He was an incredible help for me.

John Wilson was our director at that time. It was hilarious because John and Sean were very close friends but when that game started, boy, they'd go at it, head to head. It was unbelievable. Sean would be yelling at him, he'd be yelling at Sean. John was funny because he had no patience for bad baseball. We would come on the air and if the first pitch of the game wasn't a strike, he'd get in my ear and say, "Here we go!" It was fun to work with those guys. They were really important during my development as a broadcaster.

Of course, our camera crew at Fenway is the best in the business. They don't miss anything. I said in my anniversary speech to celebrate my 30th season as a broadcaster, "When you walk by a camera guy at Fenway Park, you should really thank them because we get the best shots of anybody in baseball." I really believe that. They're out there in the elements and it's freezing cold in the spring and it's hot in the summer, then cold again in the fall. But these guys don't give an inch. They're the best and I love being around them. I love the opportunity to sit down at dinner with them and talk a little bit about things other than baseball.

It's just a nice feeling to be in a group where you feel like you're part of a family that has been together for so long and works so closely together. It's a comfort level that you enjoy knowing that these people have your back.

I've always said that I don't think in 31 years I've ever had a harsh word with anyone in the truck. I just don't believe in that. I'm proud of that and I treat those people, I hope, with the most respect that I could possibly treat anyone with. In my opinion, they work so hard and they just don't get the credit that they deserve. Their names are always recognized at the end of the show, but they deserve more than that because they're invaluable to what we do.

Another aspect of the audio is the work that the audio folks do with our sideline reporter, Guerin Austin. Mark Wilcox is generally either in the booth with us or with Guerin on the sidelines, running around as she's getting interviews and making sure her audio's working. Chris Naccini usually replaces Peter when he's not there. Those guys are also big Beatles fans. Sometimes if we're in the booth together before a game, they'll put some Beatles music on the computer and we'll sing.

When we finish a game at the end of a series, that camera crew has to break down all the gear. That's another two hours of work after the game is over that nobody knows about.

Of course, there's also the on-air talent.

Tom Caron, our pre- and postgame host and a former sideline reporter for us, is simply the best. And he's a good friend of mine. He's so versatile. He holds together those shows incredibly well. He's multi-talented. He can do anything. If he has to fill in to do play-by-play for a game, he can do that. He's done games on radio. He does incredible interviews prior to games live from the field. He was an excellent sideline reporter. Even these days, he'll occasionally fill in for Guerin and it's like he never left that job.

Tom works so well with a number of postgame analysts. He gets to know their personalities. You've got to know what they're willing to talk about and how they talk about things. He does a fabulous job at that and bringing out the best in each guest.

I have a tremendous amount of respect for Tom. He's been a fixture at NESN for a long time. I think it's like a second home for him. He's a workaholic. You ask him a question, he's got the answer.

We've had a few sideline reporters during my years in the booth. It's a very, very difficult job because they're the ones who are in the clubhouse prior to the game, getting sound they can put together for a pregame show. They're the ones who have to come up with ideas for segments during the broadcast that are relevant to the game. They're the ones who have to go in and deal with players, win or lose, after the game and get sound for the postgame show and for other shows that we have on NESN.

Our current reporter, Guerin Austin, has come a long way in a few years. You can see the improvement over the last three or four years that she's been with us. You can see that her comfort level is much higher now than it was early in her career, which is understandable.

One thing that Guerin and I have in common is we both like to dance. We have had some videos from the booth where we'll be humming or singing a song, then all of a sudden, we'll break out in a dance and she takes a picture of it and puts it on Twitter. It's crazy stuff like that. We do a lot of singing and a lot of dancing in the booth.

We had Jenny Dell for a while and she eventually married third baseman Will Middlebrooks. She was also very good, very smooth on the air. For those reporters, it's like "3, 2, 1, you're on the air!"

right in the middle of a game and they've got to get out their information very, very quickly so we can get back to the action. Jenny always made her reports relevant to what was going on in the game or with the team.

We also had Hazel Mae for a while, who's gone back to Toronto and is a superstar up there. She was very popular in Boston, went to MLB Network and then back to Sportsnet in Toronto, where she's a huge star and covers the Blue Jays. Hazel was a pro and had a tremendous way about her on the air that made her a favorite here. She did great interviews and presented them in a very entertaining way. Again, she was great at her job, which is why she received so many national offers.

I loved Tina Cervasio. She had that New York accent. She pulled no punches. She was great. She was New York tough. There was no pushing Tina around at all. She's gone on to New York to have a very good career. We get a chance to see her every once in a while when we're at Yankee Stadium. She'll pop in to say hello and it's always good to see her. She was another reporter who had a good sense for news and what was pertinent at the time. She wanted to tackle bigger, tougher stories. That was in her DNA and that was really a huge trait of hers that really stuck out. Her interviews were always well thought out and she asked good questions. She knew baseball and that really came out immediately.

You just knew from the outset that Heidi Watney was going to be a superstar. She's at MLB Network now and she can do whatever she wants. She's that good. When Heidi first came in, I think that she had an awful lot to learn but she picked it up very quickly. While it's a job that doesn't seem to have a long shelf life, it was obvious that other networks were looking at her and following her work with the hopes that they could hire her away. Heidi has been very successful and is now married with a baby and working.

It's always fun to see where these young people have gone and what they've become. When you're doing the job in Boston and you're young and you're new to the business, it's tough because everybody gets criticized. It takes a while to settle in and grow that thick skin that you need. I think when their ability to put on a good hit or a good interview comes together, they gain more confidence.

I also think it's important that they learn the game. The way they learn the game is by being around the players, listening to what we have to say on TV, working with the producer and the director of the show, and really learning the game of baseball. That's probably the toughest part for them. Knowing the ins and outs, the proper language to use, how to ask a question after a game. There's nothing more boring than someone who asks the same questions in every interview after a game. Every situation is different, and I think it takes a while for them to feel that comfort level where they can spread their wings a little bit and jump out and ask the question that needs to be asked.

I think that's always an incredible learning experience for someone who's new, especially coming into this market, because you're here one day and there's already somebody criticizing you. I'm just thankful I've been able to meet and work with so many amazing and talented people.

CHAPTER 13

REMY INC.

P eople always want to know how I got started on all the marketing and business ventures I participate in. It was by pure luck really. I remember when the old regime—John Harrington was the CEO—came to me back in 2002 and said they were having a Wally the Green Monster bean bag giveaway. But they were concerned that because it was on a school day and they didn't know what kind of a crowd they were going to get. So, they asked me to push this promotion for the kids in school. If we got more than 25,000 people in the stands, my reward was to get a free dinner.

That's pretty much what started it.

Every day I'd build up that Wally's day was coming up and you get a miniature Green Monster and all this stuff. Of course, at that time it wasn't very well-received at Fenway at all. They had never seen a mascot there, you know? And the first time Wally appeared he got booed. I wasn't crazy about it myself when Wally debuted on April 13, 1997. I didn't think it fit Boston.

I must admit, it's one of the few times that anyone in the Red Sox organization had ever asked me to really push something during a broadcast. I believe that day they did reach their goal of 25,000 plus. However, I do know that I never received a dinner.

Now, you've got to remember, this was the real hot time with the Red Sox—2003 through 2005. It started right before the old regime left and the new regime—John Henry, Tom Werner, and Larry Lucchino—came in. Ratings on TV were at an all-time high. It was the miracle age of the Red Sox, really, as far as ratings and interest in the team. We were getting 18s in ratings almost every night. People were excited that the team had a legitimate chance to finally beat the Yankees.

My business partner is John O'Rourke, who had been the CEO of a few prominent companies in his day. He came up with the idea of starting a website to sell autographed scorecards and Wally seemed to be a good addition. We kind of took the idea and ran with it. I would autograph the Wally dolls and people would purchase them online. The thing went absolutely bananas. A fan sent an Adirondack chair to the ballpark and I ended up putting Wally in the chair between myself and Don Orsillo, and that became a fixture for a long time. It felt uncomfortable in a way, because here we are sitting with a doll on a chair between us, but the people seemed to like it. I'm sure there were people who hated it but I think most people liked it.

I wound up writing five books on Wally and his adventures.

As we got this website going, all kinds of ideas started to occur to John. At that time, I was probably as popular as I'd ever been. We started selling "RemDawg" T-shirts. These T-shirts were selling, these autographed Wally bean bags were selling, my autographed scorecards from the games were selling. We were selling a "Dial-a-Dawg" service where I would record the outgoing message for someone's answering machine. For example, "This is Jerry Remy. John and Mary aren't home right now. Please call back." This was very successful for about three years. There was a variety of merchandise. It was addictive. The only regret I have looking back is it felt a little unprofessional to be promoting it during the broadcasts the way I did. For example, I would say, "Go to TheRemyReport.com." On Friday nights I used to have this thing where I'd give away 10 free T-shirts. Well, that would draw hundreds of thousands of hits on the website. And they'd go on and see if they won a free T-shirt, and if they didn't, they'd buy some other stuff anyway.

It started out where it was myself; my wife, Phoebe; my business partner, John; and his wife, Kathy, doing all the packing. We couldn't keep up with it, so we eventually had to hire some help. We'd be in the basement of the O'Rourkes' condo filling orders.

We had tons and tons of these miniature Wally dolls that I had to sign and we shipped them everywhere. The same thing with the scorecards. People would request scorecards from a particular game, as well as a personalized message, anything from "My first game at Fenway," to "How about this home run," or "Best wishes to my girl-friend." It became like a full-time job. It was pretty remarkable. Sean McDonough was great. He'd go along with it. He'd pump it up and he'd make fun of it. It was all in good fun.

Then when the Red Sox won in 2004, the business went abso-lutely insane. I was signing all the scorecards of the complete series from the playoffs through the Yankees series through the World Series. We were selling packages of the whole playoffs.

I never got any complaints from the Red Sox or NESN, but it just got to a point where I thought it had become too much. I said to myself, "Shut up, Jerry. If they want something, they know where to go." I just couldn't keep promoting it on the air. I'm sure there were many people who said, "Will you shut up about this website?"

I have Sean McDonough to thank for my nickname. We often called the 2003 team "Dirt Dogs" because those guys played the game hard, guys like Trot Nixon who played hard and got their uni-forms dirty. For me, Trot was a throwback to my generation, where we had guys like Butch Hobson and Rick Burleson and Carlton Fisk, guys who were tough. Sean just came out one day and called me "RemDawg" on the air. It just took off. All of a sudden, I'm the RemDawg and everyone was calling me that. I didn't know my name was Jerry Remy anymore. I thought I was just the RemDawg.

Now when I go to sign things, people want me to sign it "Jerry Remy 'RemDawg.'" So, it's stuck with me and it's kind of cool to have a nickname like that. But the big thing is that the fans during the 2003-05 era were beside themselves with this club, because for the first time in 100 years, they had a chance to do something, and they did it. And I benefitted. John and I were stunned. Of course, we knew it wasn't going to last forever. But I knew I had to tone it back. I just felt like it became too much. At times I felt like a salesman instead of an analyst, and I felt that was wrong.

We still have the Remy Report site and we still get plenty of hits on it. We still get some sales of different things, but not nearly what it was like at that particular hot time. But it's been good. We've added Facebook and Instagram since then. Twitter is huge for us, a great tool for me to get information out to my fans.

The Jerry Remy restaurants really started at Fenway, not far from where the NESN pregame show is outside Gate D. They put a hot dog stand out there and called it RemDawg's. The Red Sox called us about it and we made a deal. It was pretty exciting for me to walk outside and there's people buying my hot dogs. We had a lot of activity out there.

That went strong for a couple of years, and then we decided to go into the restaurant business, which today I think was a mistake. The restaurant business is a very, very tough business. Our first location was at Terminal C at Logan Airport, and it's the only restaurant I'm still involved with. We opened one near Fenway, which was magical through the summer but it was dead through the winter. It was hard. You had to make all your money through one stretch of the season, and then make that last for 12 months out of the year. We eventually got out of that. We opened a few others, but we just got out of all of them except for the airport location.

I've got to tell you, it was kind of a rush to walk into your own restaurant before a game or after a game and see tons of people in there drinking and eating and having a good time. But now I only focus on being the best analyst I can be in the booth.

CHAPTER 14
THE CHANGES
IN BASEBALL

L et me preface my comments by saying that I'm not one of those guys who feels like the era you played in is the best era. But there's no question there have been major changes in the game of baseball since the time I was playing.

One of the things that is most evident is the information that these players have at their disposal today that we didn't have. They call it analytics and it's become a big part of the game. I would have died to have just a fraction of what's available to the players today, through the analytics, through the video, through everything they have at their disposal. And the key to any of that is taking what's available to you and taking what is important to you and putting it into practice. I think you can get overloaded at times with stuff, but the fact is the more information you can gather, obviously the better it is. I think that's one of the biggest changes I've seen.

When I was a player, we'd go over the advanced scouting report in the meetings and it was kind of a joke. It was stuff like, this guy will go the opposite field, or this guy will pull the ball on this count. They were very, very bare-boned meetings. And then when you'd ask about the pitchers we'd be facing, they'd say they hadn't seen them. The ability today to go on video and watch everything that a guy has ever done in his life and what he's done to you has to be an enormous help. Any time a relief pitcher comes in the game, immediately the player goes over and can look over a report on them, and they're able to even look at videos on them. For us, it was remembering what somebody had done to you. If it was a guy you had never seen, you had no clue about him. Now there's video on everyone, even a young minor league kid. It's remarkable.

The same is true on defense. The positioning of players, the shifts, everything is down to such to a science. We basically had to go on our own memory of how we played a particular player in the past. Very rarely would we ever shift on anybody. I think the first shift that I saw was when we were playing the Kansas City Royals, and Jim Rice was having this monster year in 1978. Whitey Herzog actually put Freddie Patek, their shortstop, out in the outfield. So, they had four outfielders. We were like, what's going on? We couldn't believe there were four outfielders. I remember when Carlton Fisk went over to the White Sox, we'd shift on him. And as a second baseman, I felt like a fish out of water being on the other side of the infield. Now it's just common. They practice shifts, and I'm all for them.

There's a lot of talk about eliminating shifts or modifying shifts. I don't see why they have to do that. I honestly believe that if you're in fair territory, it's open game. They're leaving you some part of the field to deal with, so learn how to deal with it. So, I'm not against the shifts at all. It's so commonplace now that, to me, it's interesting to watch how they shift on different players and how they shift even between pitches on where they locate players.

For example, if they shifted the right side against a left-handed hitter, they want their best defensive player in a position where he hits the ball the most. So that's why you'll see, with a couple of strikes, a guy shifted to a different position. I find it intriguing. I know the hitters hate it, but the fact is it's proven effective. I don't think it's bad for baseball. I think it's up to the players to adjust to what's happening to them.

Another difference between generations is I think the game was a little bit more intimidating from a pitcher's point of view. I'm not saying I totally agree with this, but if there were back-to-back home runs, you could pretty much guarantee the next guy was going down. There were a lot more knockdown pitches and brushback pitches than there are in today's game. A guy like myself, who bunted a lot, if I bunted against a pitcher who was pretty upset with me, well, the next time, they'd shoot for my legs because they knew that was my game. So, there was a lot more intimidation from pitchers. If you had a 4-for-4 night going, you knew that fifth time you were going down, either then or the next day.

I remember playing against the Red Sox when I was with the Angels. Dick Williams was our manager and he always loved to rub it into the Red Sox as much as he could after they fired him in 1969. We didn't have a team that was capable of beating up on the Red Sox, but we had a 6–0 lead late in the game, and he put a squeeze play on with me. A squeeze play with a 6–0 lead? That's against the unwritten rules. The next day, Roger Moret was pitching for the Red Sox, and the first pitch was up over my head. The second pitch was up over my head. The third pitch was behind me. Finally, I'm saying to myself, just hit me and get this over with. And finally, he walked me. He couldn't hit me. He just walked me. And when I got back to the dugout, Williams said, "Well, I guess I got you thrown at."

So, there was more of that kind of stuff going on.

We also have new rules now protecting second basemen, which we call the Chase Utley Rule after Utley wiped out Ruben Tejada in Game 2 of the 2016 National League division series between the Mets and Dodgers. In the seventh inning of that game, Utley slid late and past the bag into Tejada in a clear attempt to break up a double play. Tejeda suffered a broken leg and the rule was changed to try and prevent that from happening again.

That type of wipeout slide was commonplace when I played. Now, middle infielders can be very comfortable in that situation. Guys used to be able to come in and do whatever they wanted to do. I've got snapshots of guys like Hal McRae just taking me out to lunch at second base, where today those would be called double plays. I wish we had that rule when I played. It would have been so much more comfortable playing second base.

The other big change is the use of the starting pitchers. I think that the idea of complete games is pretty much history in baseball. If he gives you five or six innings, you start going to the bullpen right away. The bullpens are much, much stronger and sophisticated than they were when I played.

When I was playing, you kind of hoped that you didn't see the same pitcher four times, because that meant he was beating you. On the other hand, sometimes you felt more comfortable seeing him for the fourth time rather than seeing a pitcher only twice and then here come different guys out of the bullpen. I think it's a little bit harder to get a comfort level today against pitching than it was in the past because the hitter sees so many different pitchers. But they have the information to back it up, so it's kind of a two-way street.

The whole idea of playing for one run doesn't exist now unless it's like the eighth or ninth inning in a ballgame. I remember when managing the Twins, Gene Mauch, and even when Dick Williams was managing the Angels, we would bunt in the first inning to try to get a man on second base with one out to try to take the early lead in the game. You don't see that anymore.

It's lift and launch now. It's trying to put two runs on the board instead of one, or multiple runs on the board. I'm not going to say whether the change is for the best or not. Like I said, I'm not a guy who thinks my era was the best. I just think they're all good.

One change that does bother me is all of the strikeouts. And it comes from this new lift-and-launch approach to hitting and trying to put multiple runs on the board at once. There's no such thing as cutting down your swing with two strikes. I mean, that used to be a major part of our game plan. If you had two strikes on you, you'd try to avoid the strikeout because nothing good comes out of a strike-out. If you can put the ball in play, something good can happen. You could get on by a base hit, you could get on by an error. There are ways to get on base. We were always taught to shorten up and try to make contact and move the ball the other way, and just to battle not to strike out. But now, you basically see no change in a two-strike swing versus a 2-0 swing.

Things go in cycles, and I don't know how long this cycle will last. I really don't. Baseball continues to change all the time. But we're in a cycle now where it seems like it's home run or strikeout, and it's very rare to see a guy with two strikes on him shorten up on his swing and try to just hook a ball the other way for a base hit. It's almost like they'd rather take a strikeout and still go for the home run. So that's a big change in the game today.

And hit-and-runs, well, you don't see nearly as many of those. It was guaranteed, if you were facing a sinker-ball pitcher, that you were going to play hit-and-run almost all game because sinker-ball pitchers induced a lot of ground balls and you wanted to stay away from double plays. You'd see a lot more movement on the bases than you see today. But I don't think there are as many sinker-ball pitchers as there were when I played. Most guys have power arms, as they call them, and there are more strikeout guys than when I was playing.

I don't mind the changes as much as some of the players of my era, maybe because I've always stayed around the game. I went from player to broadcaster, so I've lived the changes. I've grown with them. When players of my generation look at the game today, they don't think it's as good as when we played.

Another huge change is the length of games. I'm all for a pitch clock. If you look at video from that '78 playoff game, you see Ron Guidry getting the ball and throwing it. And the hitters didn't leave the box. If they left the box, it was generally one foot out of the box and you'd take a practice swing or something or pick up some dirt, then step right back in there.

As a matter of fact, in those days, there were certain pitchers who, if you didn't get in the box, they'd walk up to you and say, "Get in the goddamn box." Same thing if you were digging a hole. For example, remember the old story about Bob Gibson, where some player got in there and was digging his comfort level with his back foot, and Gibson walked up to him and said something like, "You better dig that hole, because I'm going to bury you in it the next pitch."

The pitchers didn't like when hitters took a long time. There were very few hitters who took a long time in the box. Fisk was certainly one of them and Mike Hargrove was like a human rain delay, but most guys, they'd just get in the box. So, the reason games are longer is a combination of the tempo of a pitcher and also the tempo of a hitter.

Somehow, they've got to get those things to work together, and that's why I think there should be a pitch clock in the game. We time guys sometimes who take 40 seconds between pitches. Ridiculous.

I think Major League Baseball has improved things by limiting visits to the mound, because that was getting way out of hand. And quite frankly, pitchers, the ones I've talked to, don't like visits to the mound. They want to focus on the game. I've known pitchers when I played who never wanted the pitching coach or the manager coming out to the mound.

Sometimes TV has a part in it. There's no question about that. You've got the TV timeouts that are extended and pretty long, especially in the national games but even in the local games.

It's coming to a point where, when you go to a ballpark and you have a 7:05 PM start, and if you get out of there at 10:00 or 10:05, a three-hour game, you think you've had a fast game. Our games, I think, if you looked back on them, they were around 2:20 or 2:30. It makes a big difference, I think, to the fans and the players. I think players prefer a faster-paced game. I'm certain fans do.

I feel for kids now because when we were kids, there so many day games. We'd listen to them in school, we'd go home and listen to the rest of it or watch it if it was on TV, and there was interest.

Now, in nationally televised games, first pitch is like 8:37 at night. Well, I mean, the best part of the game is coming at 11:30, midnight. What kids are going to be able to watch that? They worry about young people losing interest in the game? Well, I'm tired of watching a game starting at 8:37 at night. It's ridiculous. I get it's all about TV ratings and advertising, and I understand that. But if you're looking to keep kids interested in the game, pick up the pace of the game and start them a bit earlier.

This generation of kids are—how should I say this?—things happen quickly for them. They are part of the video game generation. They get information on their phones as it happens and I think they would much prefer to see a faster-paced game. I think baseball has to quicken the pace to hold younger viewers.

Then we have the ballparks. So many of them when I played were the cookie-cutter ones, multi-sport facilities and not necessarily built for baseball. The newer ones are built for home runs.

Camden Yards is a great example. It was the first of the modern stadiums and I think one of the most beautiful parks in baseball, but it's a place where it's fairly easy to hit home runs. I think a lot of the new ballparks, which are absolutely gorgeous, are built to improve offense in the game.

My generation played in some pretty crappy places. I remember Cleveland's Municipal Stadium, and that big ballpark held 80,000 people and 6,000 people would be there. Terrible places. They've done a great job with these new facilities that they've put up. It's beautiful to watch games, all the seating is very good. You don't have seats facing in different directions, like at the Metrodome in Minneapolis, which was built for football, and you'd have seats behind home plate, facing out toward right field. It was ridiculous.

Playing conditions on the fields themselves are so much better than what we had. You know, the mixture of the dirt on the infield, it's just perfect now. I'm sure there are some that are better than others, but when I was playing, there were a handful of fields you went to and you said, wow, this is a nice infield. Now the grounds crews come out and they drag the rakes over the infield every three innings. When I played they'd come out and drag it kind of half-assed by the fifth inning, once a game, so you were playing on a chopped-up infield for most of the game.

The other big difference is the way injuries are dealt with.

They immediately put you on the injured list, which is now 10 days. There was no such thing, when I played, as going down to the minor leagues for a rehab assignment. It was like, when you were ready to play, you were back. You'd recover and get back into shape with the major league team. And guys in those days were afraid to be out of the lineup because the money wasn't what it is today, and you were afraid of losing your job. You didn't want to be sitting on the sidelines. You wanted to play through some injuries.

But they're paying these guys so much money now that teams are extremely cautious with them, which I understand. It doesn't bother me, but I think times have changed, especially financially, and the owners are protecting their investments as much as they possibly can now, especially with pitchers. In the past, that wasn't the case. Guys would be out there pitching with bad arms and who knew if they needed Tommy John surgery? It didn't exist in those days.

I missed time with my knee problems, but I always worried about keeping my job. Going on the injured list was kind of a big deal back then, and now it's just kind of normal. The manager calls you in, you go on a 10-day list, okay, be back in 10 days, take a little break, and they're back in the starting lineup. Or they go down for a rehab assignment. Sometimes these rehab assignments drive me crazy. The guy's making four appearances at the minor league level, where there's really no need to do that. It used to be that, once you were off the injured list, you were back in the lineup. When you said you were ready to go, you were ready to go, and you played. So that's a big change in the game right now, too.

Another change is the way the manager interacts with the players. There was no such thing as "communication" back then.

The old-time managers could never survive in the game today. They were the final authority figure. What they said went. You didn't get to question anything. They were it. And you were afraid of them. It was their way or the highway. So that has changed dramatically and I think it's changed for the better, to be quite honest with you, because you can sit down and have a conversation with a manager now.

I think Alex Cora was a great example of that in 2018. He was always involved with the players in some way, shape, or form, every day, going and sitting with them in the clubhouse. You never saw that in my day, a manager come and sit in the clubhouse. You'd walk by their office and half the time you wouldn't get a hello, or you'd just look and see if your name was in the lineup.

And there were a lot of fines that would hurt your wallet because you weren't making a lot of money. If you didn't make contact on two strikes, you'd get fined for striking out. Just different kinds of little piddly things like that. As great as those managers were—and there were great, great managers—it was their way or the highway. I'm sure certain guys were different, but not to the extent they are today.

Rookie manager Alex Cora pushed all the right buttons, leading the Red Sox to another World Series title in 2018. (AP Images)

I'll never forget a conversation I had with Dick Williams. He was with Seattle, and it was right at the end of his career. I was broadcasting at the time, and he was a guy I always admired because he was the first manager I played for, and I thought that he taught me more baseball in one year than anyone else, although in a very tough way. I remember going up to him in Seattle, and he just shook his head and he said, "I got to get out. The game's changed so much. It's not for me anymore." He was kind of at that transition point where managers were starting to get closer to the players, and that wasn't the world he had come from. Guys like Dick, Earl Weaver, Gene Mauch, all had a different way of going about things. They'd have no hesitation in sending your ass back to Triple-A.

I think that's what might have happened to Bobby Valentine in Boston in 2012. After the team fired Terry Francona, it seemed like Valentine was the best choice for the job. Bobby confuses me because I remember him as a player. I played with him for a very, very brief time with the Angels, and he was pretty much the same guy as a manager. Now, I don't know what he was like with the Mets and Rangers, but when he came here he just didn't relate to the players.

He'd been out of the game as a manager for about 10 years and I think the game had changed and Bobby didn't change with it. Maybe the years in Japan made him different, I don't know. But he wasn't close to the players, and then obviously the players didn't like him.

They didn't like him really in spring training because he started to change a lot of things, with cutoffs and relays and how they were going to do things. A lot of players felt like, what, is he trying to reinvent the game here? That's kind of the way they felt about him right out of the shoot. And I said, uh-oh, this may not be good as time rolls on.

And I liked Bobby. I liked him a lot. I liked his enthusiasm. He had a passion for the game. But he was very strong-minded in things that he believed in, which didn't really jell with the players in this particular timeframe.

After the collapse in September of 2011, I felt they had a team that had a chance to win in 2012, and I was against bringing in a rookie manager at that time. I thought they needed a veteran guy. But it didn't work out that way, and I was quite surprised by that.

I guess the only thing you can really count on in baseball is that, like life, it's always evolving!

CHAPTER 15
DEPRESSION

Threnthe first time I battled depression, I was under a lot of stress from issues at home.

I had been used to doing an 81-game schedule with NESN. The 1997 season was the first year that I did all of the games. Basically, that's how it started. I don't think I had suffered from anything like that in the past. I got really sick with a bad chest cold in Baltimore but went on to Cleveland with the team on July 18. I went to do my usual stuff in the clubhouse, which I did before every game. I was heading to the elevator to go back to the booth when all of a sudden, I started to feel flushed and sweaty. I felt pain shooting down my arm and I thought I was having a heart attack.

I rushed back to the clubhouse and told the trainer at that time that something was wrong. I laid down on the trainer's table and he called the Cleveland team doctor. The doctor came right over and checked my heart and said that it was fine. He said, "You may have had a panic attack."

I said, "A panic attack? I've never had one in my life!" I ended up going back to the hotel that night; I didn't do the game.

I continued to have these episodes. They just kept happening over and over again. Every place I would have one, if I even thought about that place afterward, I'd have another attack. I remember going to the ballpark and going to the booth and immediately having a panic attack because I had experienced one there previously. Even during the middle of a game, it would start up again. All this time, I was still working and doing all the games.

I got really claustrophobic. I was afraid to drive because I didn't want to get caught in traffic. I needed space between my car and the car in front of me, so I could get out of the way if I started to have an attack. This continued throughout the whole season.

They got so bad, and I was having them so consistently, that they sent me into depression. I just felt lifeless; I couldn't do anything. I didn't want to get out of bed in the morning, and I didn't want to get up the next morning because I didn't want to go through another day like I just had. It was horrific.

I finally went to see a psychiatrist who confirmed that I was having panic attacks. I asked, "How the hell do you get rid of them?" I started therapy but I'm not much of a talker, so I wasn't buying into it. I was actually having panic attacks while I was talking to him about having them. After trying deep breathing exercises, none of which worked for me, he prescribed some medication, Xanax. I was apprehensive about taking Xanax, so I'd only take the pills occasionally. I was told, "When you start to have a panic attack, take the Xanax." But that wasn't helping because, by then, it would be too late. At the same time, I was scared because this was interfering with my daily work regimen.

It got to a point where I remember getting up one morning, looking out the window at my home in Weston, and felt like jumping out the bathroom window. I didn't want to go on like this, I couldn't do it. It was just a brief thought; I wasn't going to kill myself. But it got so bad, that's how I felt.

I went to another doctor who told me, "Don't wait until you start getting a panic attack to take your medication. Take two pills every four hours, that will help you keep yourself under control." That's what I did. At the same time, I started to take an antidepressent medication, Zoloft. It's trial and error finding the correct medication and sometimes can take up to six weeks before there is any improvement.

All this was going on during the season, but I made it through. As I got on a routine of taking my medications, I was okay. I wasn't having panic attacks as much and I started to feel much better.

The second bout of depression was after I had my first cancer surgery in November 2008. The lower lobe of my right lung was removed. Everything was going well but in early January I developed a cough and was having trouble with acid reflux. With the doctor's blessings, I went to Aruba with my wife, as I had just about every off-season. As the vacation went on, the acid reflux got worse and I couldn't keep anything down. I was admitted to Mass General the day I returned from Aruba. I had developed an infection. My surgeon, Dr. Wright, and my pulmonologist, Dr. O'Donnell, were very concerned. Dr. Wright said, "I may have to operate again to drain the infected area." They finally decided on draining the area with tubes and using antibiotics, so I was in the hospital for a week receiving IV treatments to clear the infection.

I came out of that fine and I went to spring training, but I was very weak. It was the first time that I had cancer surgery and then I had the infection on top of it. I was probably not ready to go, but I started the season anyway. We had to make a West Coast trip early in the year. On the way out to California, I was fine. The next day—April 10, 2009—I woke up in Anaheim and I was completely zonked, I was out of it. It was the same day the young Angels pitcher, Nick Adenhart, died in a car accident.

I fell into depression again because I was concerned that I wouldn't be able to do my job. I continued on the road trip but I was totally miserable. I didn't want to go to work; I couldn't wait to get back home. I made it through the next homestand. I was a bit better but another road trip was coming.

In early May, we traveled from Cleveland down to Tampa. I got so bad in Tampa that I couldn't get out of my chair. I called Russ Kenn, who was our producer at the time, and said, "Russ, I'm a mess. I can't leave my room."

He said, "What do you mean, you can't leave your room?"

I said, "I can't, I'm totally depressed. I'm afraid to go to the ballpark."

He called Phoebe and she flew down to Tampa to get me. I was in such a state that I didn't want to leave my room and I didn't want to fly home. I didn't want to be seen. I suggested to my wife that we rent a car to drive back home.

She said, "What? What are you talking about? I don't think that's a good idea."

I said, "I can't fly. I just want to drive; I think I can drive."

She reasoned with me and we ended up flying home.

When we did get back home, I had to call NESN and tell them that I couldn't keep doing this. I was definitely battling depression again. This episode lasted for approximately six weeks. Sean McGrail and Joel Feld from NESN came to my house and they said, "You know, why don't you come to the ballpark? It might help you break out of this."

I replied, "Come to the ballpark? I can't even leave the house. I have no desire to go to the ballpark. I can't do it. I can't leave the house!" This happened a couple of times. Eventually, I did get to the ballpark. I got a nice ovation from the crowd when they introduced me and that did make me feel better. However, it didn't fix my problem. I still couldn't face returning to the booth to broadcast the games.

The decision was made to start me on a new antidepressant medication, Lexapro. I realized then and there that I would probably need this type of medication for the rest of my life. I haven't missed a day since. Thankfully, even with my personal and health issues, I haven't had another problem with depression.

It's an awful thing to go through. In the past, I don't think depression got enough attention. People were ashamed to admit that they had a problem. They didn't want to be labeled as being "crazy." Things have progressed and having a mental health issue is no longer a stigma. It's a disease that can be successfully treated.

I take my medications faithfully and I haven't had panic attacks or depression in years. Those were two periods in my life that were really, really bad. I developed a new appreciation for people who suffered with these issues. Until it affects you personally, you can't imagine how intimidating and debilitating these conditions are. Those two episodes of dealing with depression hit me hard.

In many ways, it was worse than cancer. The cancer was always caught early enough where they could do something about it and so you felt okay about that. But the depression was something you just had no idea where it came from. There was no family history of it. I never knew when I played that I may suffer from this. I was always an anxious person, but to develop panic attacks and to have that sudden depression was stunning to me. It was just at a stage in my life where I never expected anything like that to happen.

Looking back on it, I think maybe there were signs earlier in my life. For example, I was really moody during my playing days and shortly after I was done playing. I would be in just a horrible mood for no reason at all. I didn't know why. I'd just get out of bed and I'd be totally miserable. This would go on for three or four days and then I'd be fine. There was no reason for me to be that way, but I never gave that a second thought. I thought it was just my personality. This used to pop up once every couple of months. I thought I was just in a bad mood. Now when I look back on it, I haven't had a day like that since I've been free of depression. I could never explain to myself why I felt that way and then it would go away, and I'd be fine. It could've been the prelude to some of these things that happened to me later in life, but I was never diagnosed with anything, and, quite frankly, never had it checked out.

My wife had to suffer through my mood swings as well. I remember one time, I had been miserable for days and I came home after a bad game and I snapped at one of the kids for no reason at all. She had had enough and she laid me out.

Phoebe said, "It isn't our fault that you stink! You're going to cut this crap out because I'm not putting up with it and you're not taking it out on the kids!"

Needless to say, I never did that again. I'm just thankful I was able to get it under control.

CHAPTER 16
JARED

Thus is the chapter I never wanted to write. This is the chapter that Nick Cafardo and I decided to save for last during our deliberations for this book.

There are so many legalities involved, so many lives were affected. It's not an easy topic for me to talk about. There isn't a day that goes by that I don't think about what happened. I know it will be that way the rest of my life.

The cancer, the anxiety, the depression—nothing compares to this.

It's so hard to write this: my son Jared brutally murdered his fiancée, Jennifer Martel, on August 15, 2013.

I found out while I was in Toronto, where we were finishing up a road trip. I was actually on the bus heading to the airport when I got a call from my wife, Phoebe. I knew it couldn't be good news, because she never calls at that time. I picked up the phone and she let me know that something had happened between Jared and Jen, and that Jen was in bad shape.

Phoebe said, "I'll call you back when I know more," and hung up. Just as we were rushing to get on the plane, she called back and said, "Jen died." That's all the conversation we had because the plane was ready to take off. I sat on the plane in total shock. I don't remember the flight. I don't even remember taking my seat. I was in a complete daze. All I could think about was what had happened at home.

By the time we landed, I knew that my son had been arrested and that he was responsible for the terrible act. I walked up to Jack McCormick, the team's traveling secretary, and let him know that something terrible had happened and that, as a result, there might be some chaos around me and the organization. The news was already out in the media, but when I arrived at Fenway, there was no one there.

It was and continues to be, by far, the most horrible day of our lives. There's not a day that goes by that we don't think about Jen and what a heinous act was committed by our son. Two families were ruined, and a beautiful woman who was so full of life was gone.

The next day we were immediately crushed by the media, which we totally expected. Media trucks were set up everywhere in our development. It was awful; we couldn't go anywhere near a window.

We received a call from one of our close friends who suggested that we spend time at their home, away from Boston, to collect our thoughts. We spent three days there, trying to come to grips with what had occurred. We were absolutely distraught.

More and more details were coming out about what had happened. Talking to our lawyer, there was no question that Jared was going to be charged with first-degree murder.

The trial date was set for the fall of 2014, but in May of that year, Jared decided to plead guilty to the charges against him. He told Phoebe that a trial would be a circus and that he didn't want to put his family through that. He said, "I did this, this is my fault, this is my responsibility."

He made his decision knowing that he would spend the rest of his life in prison. He wasn't looking for an out. No one was looking to get him out of anything. There was no out for anyone involved. We were just going through the legal process and dealing with everything that came with it. We were trying to deal with our grief as well as protect and do what was best for our grandchildren. What I do know is that it was a tragedy and, for our grandchildren, a terrible, life-altering event.

So, now, Jared spends his life in prison. We talk to him when he calls, we visit, write letters. His life has changed in the worst possible way. It's just so hard, and it's something our family has to deal with daily.

For Jen's family, their daughter is gone. What do you say to them? There are no words. Jen was the sweetest, most loving person you could ever meet. She was a gem.

And our son is responsible for taking her life. That's not an easy thing to accept. It's the guilt that's consuming. We will live with this tragedy for the rest of our lives. You wouldn't wish this on your worst enemy. It's absolutely horrible.

Our grandchildren have rebounded as well as can be expected. I have as much respect and adoration for my grandson, Dominik, as anyone I know. He's an incredible young man. With what he's had to go through in his life, to turn out the way that he's turned out right now, it just makes me so proud. We get to be with our 10-year-old granddaughter, Arianna, who is a sweet, loving child. She is special; she is our little angel.

What bothered me so much after the tragedy was the criticism of my wife. I heard comments like, "How can she be a responsible grandmother when she can't even raise her own kids?" Of course, this narrative took off on the talk shows. It was nasty; it went above and beyond. I promised her that I'd never do another talk show, and I have kept my promise.

The criticism lasted for months. It was just relentless and cruel. People would offer opinions on whether I should ever work again and speculate about how I could possibly do my job knowing that my son had murdered the mother of his child, my grandchild.

I certainly had those thoughts, I really did. I thought this was going to be it. I didn't know if I could ever return to the booth.

A meeting was set up with Red Sox chairman Tom Werner, president Larry Lucchino, principal owner John Henry, NESN boss Sean McGrail, and communications director Dr. Charles Steinberg. They asked me what I wanted to do, and I said I didn't think I could go on. Honestly, I was in no condition to broadcast a game nor did

I have the desire to. They told me to do what I needed to do. They couldn't have been more understanding. I could tell that they really felt for me, that they cared for me and my family. It was agreed that I would take the rest of the year off, to attempt to get my head on straight, and come back the following year. Then Larry Lucchino kindly offered me his house in La Jolla, California, if Phoebe and I needed to get away. I never took him up on it, but the gesture was amazing. That's how much these people cared about Phoebe and me.

Sean McGrail, from NESN, was very supportive. I've said it over and over again, but the relationship I've had with Sean and Red Sox ownership, Larry included, and now Sam Kennedy, who replaced Larry as team president, has been off the charts for me.

These people have treated me like family. They have supported me through my bouts of cancer, depression, missed work, and have been nothing less than 100 percent in my corner. I'd run through a wall for them; I really would.

While Jared is our son, what he did was unforgivable.

CHAPTER 17
DEALING WITH CANCER

I thought I had bronchitis or pneumonia. I was really sick, and I went in to see Dr. Larry Ronan, who is the Red Sox team physician. He took a chest X-ray and he didn't like what he saw in the bottom of my right lung and he suggested a CT scan. I credit him with saving my life because I would have never known that I had cancer if I hadn't gone to see him. He immediately scheduled a CT scan for me. The scan result showed a suspicious spot that needed to be biopsied. The biopsy showed that, yes, the mass was cancerous, and it had to be removed.

The first time I had the cancer removed, I had a minimally invasive procedure. They took it out and that was it. There was no radiation, there was no chemotherapy. I bounced back from that surgery okay. I tried to keep it quiet. Unfortunately, I developed an infection and that's what really knocked me out to a point where it was kind of touch and go. That's the spring training where I was exhausted. I had lost a lot of weight. I was really thin. I had been accustomed to doing every game. It was like hell if I missed a game. Suddenly, I'm battling a post-op infection, I'm battling depression, I'm battling panic attacks, I'm battling cancer. It just all came crashing down on me. That was the first time.

I was scheduled for CT scans every three months. The second time it showed up, I was able to be treated with radiation. I had a week's worth of radiation that took care of the tumor. It was just five treatments. That was the second time.

The third time was the same thing. After having a normal CT scan, there was a strange spot on a follow-up scan. It required radiation again to remove this spot. I was told I would need five more treatments. I was fine after that. It wasn't long enough to make me feel fatigued or have any other side effects. The doctors told me that everything was okay for now.

The fourth time they detected another spot needing treatment, it was brutal. It was major surgery. They opened me up around my shoulder blade in order to remove the tumor. The doctors were very confident that the surgery would take care of the cancer. But two days after the surgery, they came in to let me know that the final report showed several other adjacent areas that needed to be treated. That made it a whole different ballgame. Now I would need three cycles of chemotherapy, which would be done once every three weeks. That would be followed by 27 treatments of radiation. We did all that from June of 2017 until January 15, 2018.

I was kind of wiped out after this episode because this was very intensive treatment. It took me approximately 10 weeks to completely recover after the surgery. The chemotherapy was like a rollercoaster ride. That amount of radiation took much more out of me than the previous times. I didn't realize it until I got to spring training. When you're home in the winter, you're not doing a lot of walking around. When I got to the ballpark, I started walking around the complex and I was exhausted. I decided to get up early every day to go out to the ballpark and just take little walks around the complex to increase my stamina. That seemed to help.

Finally, I thought I was out of the woods. But then I had another relapse in July of 2018. I had known that my cancer had returned for about a week, but I wanted to do the Yankees series at Fenway. I actually flew to Toronto with the team and I had intended to wait until the end of the season to deal with this latest setback. Once I got there, I thought, what am I doing? Cancer can't wait! I got my butt back home the next day to address this diagnosis.

I couldn't believe I had relapsed so quickly. My two best options for treatment were, again, surgery or radiation. This procedure would make my last surgery feel like a walk in the park. For the first time, I was really scared. Especially when the surgeon, Dr. Wright, told me that he could remove my entire right lung, which may eliminate the recurrences, but that I could die on the operating table or from complications afterward. If I survived the surgery, there were no guarantees about my quality of life. So, I decided against the surgery and opted for radiation.

The doctors were concerned with keeping me in remission. Because of a gene I have, immunotherapy alone was a long shot at successfully treating future tumors. They told me I may qualify for a clinical trial where tissue from my previous tumor would be used to create a personalized vaccine. The vaccine, in turn, allows the immunotherapy drug to work more effectively. In early November of 2018, after my last scan, I heard that I was cancer free. Later in November, I was informed that I was a match for the vaccine and was admitted into the clinical trial to prevent further recurrences.

The next step was to receive the vaccine (and immunotherapy drug) through IV therapy. I would need to receive treatment once a week for eight consecutive weeks. Because of possible side effects, I would have to be monitored for up to 10 hours on some days. That would be my schedule for January and February of 2019. I was really looking forward to that! I am through the most difficult part and am now receiving treatment once every three weeks.

When I had a couple of relapses and needed chemotherapy, I was in contact with John Farrell and he was very helpful in talking me through it. I also talked to a couple of other people who had had cancer and had been through chemotherapy; I tried to get as much feedback as I could on what to expect. Quite frankly, I found it not to be as devastating as I had anticipated. Although, make no mistake, it was a rough ride. You're emotionally high and emotionally low due to the steroid medication you take to combat the side effects of chemotherapy. Exhaustion is a factor. Just when you start feeling better, it's time for another treatment. You don't feel good for very long. I was fortunate not to have any nausea or vomiting.

My daughter, Jenna, was married on November 4, 2017. I had just finished a chemotherapy treatment a couple of weeks earlier, so I was feeling well. I was able to attend *and* enjoy our daughter's wedding; that was a gift. I was initially scheduled for one more treatment after the wedding, but the treatments were starting to affect my hearing and my liver. The doctors decided against a fourth treatment. The end result is that due to the chemotherapy, I now have to wear hearing aids.

I started as a punk smoker. I was about 16, and I just smoked and smoked and smoked. When I signed professionally with the Angels and was going off for my first spring training, I thought that would be it for smoking. You're a pro athlete now, you can't smoke. When I arrived at spring training, to my surprise, some of the coaches and players were smoking. I thought it would be against the rules to smoke in pro baseball, but it obviously was not. I figured, oh, this is strange.

Instead of stopping, I continued smoking, and I never stopped. I was addicted to it. When you're young, you don't think anything is going to happen to you. You're invincible. I basically smoked my entire life. There's no question in my mind that the cancer is due to the smoking. No doubt about that, whatsoever.

I'd say I'd average approximately a pack of Marlboro Reds a day. However, there were days when, if we had a doubleheader or I was out late at night, I could have had two packs. Over the years, I tried to quit a couple of times, but it didn't work. Truthfully, I never made a full effort to quit until recently and I have been able to stop now. Hopefully, it's not too late. I always said that it's easier to pick up the first one than to put down the last one. I don't want to preach to people about the dangers of smoking because I used to hate hearing it from others. The only thing I would say is, don't pick up that first one because it becomes awfully tough after that.

When I got to the Red Sox, we had some smokers. Cigarettes were readily available in the clubhouse for those who smoked. You'd go to a certain city, and if the clubhouse manager knew you smoked, there would be a carton of cigarettes sitting on your chair even before you arrived at the ballpark. We had quite a few closet smokers, too. They were the guys who weren't regular smokers, but during games, they'd go down and fire up between at-bats.

To this day, the first thing I want to do when I get up in the morning is have a cigarette. I've come to where, if I can get through the mornings, I'm good for the rest of the day. I don't smoke at the ballpark anymore. If I'm having a couple of glasses of wine after the game in my hotel room, I don't smoke. But it's a battle. Many times I go to sit in the lobby because I have to get out of my room. I want to smoke so badly; I've got to go where people are so I don't smoke.

I wear a nicotine patch every day. I'm not going to lie; I still want to smoke. That sounds sick considering everything I've been through but that's how addictive it is. I smoked for almost 50 years and I'm paying the price.

I think, in this day and age, kids and people in general are well informed about how bad smoking is for you. My family gets it; they've seen, up close, what I've been through. They do not smoke.

I'm not surrounded by a lot of people who smoke. I must say that, at times, when I come out of the ballpark and I start smelling those cigarettes, it's difficult. I remember when I first tried quitting, I would walk past half-filled ashtrays on tables or those ashtrays that are outside of restaurants and I'd think, man, there's still a couple of puffs on those...I could have that! That's how crazy smoking can make you.

The road trips are extremely difficult for me; I'm much better when I'm home. An off day on the road, when I didn't have anything to do, that used to be a day where I'd sit in my room and have a glass of wine and a cigarette and just unwind. I've got to really battle it now; I'm trying to do whatever I can to avoid smoking. It's weird; in the evenings, I still have my wine but I don't smoke. I thought that would bother me much more, but it doesn't. It's the mornings that are the hardest.

In the morning on the road, I get up, I'll grab a cup of coffee, I'll eat a bagel. Sometimes I'm ready to go by 10:30 AM, sitting in the lobby for a 7:00 PM game. I've just got to get out. People laugh at me because I'm sitting in the lobby so early, but I can't sit in my room. I can't do it. I try to go to places where it takes your mind off it. That's how I've been trying to handle it so far. It's not as tough at home because my wife is like a hawk. She's on me all the time.

But this is my life. I have to battle every day.

CHAPTER 18
IN CONCLUSION

If you've read this book in its entirety, you must realize by now that my life hasn't been easy. You also know that I had the good fortune to be a major league baseball player and play for my beloved Red Sox. The good times continued with a fulfilling broadcasting career that has spanned more than 30 years.

I will say this, I couldn't have done it without my life partner, my wife, Phoebe. She *is* my best friend. She's the strongest person in the world that I know. She's the rock of our family. We've been married for 44 years.

When we met, Phoebe Brum was a student at Bridgewater State College and a seasonal employee wrapping Christmas presents at Empire Men's Shop in Fall River, where I worked as a salesman in the off-season. I don't know, we just hit it off. Phoebe actually knew my mother (and sister) because some of Phoebe's friends and her niece, Heidi, took dance lessons at the studio where my mother worked. So, that was a connection. Phoebe said that when she first saw me, I reminded her of someone but that she couldn't pinpoint who. I look like my mother; I guess that explains it.

We were married in October of 1974; that was the year that I played winter ball in Mexico. Let's just say, we were not in a resort town. Phoebe was sick the entire time. It wasn't a pleasant experience for either of us, but we got through it. We've endured so much together. A baseball wife's life may look glamorous from afar but it's really not. It's kind of a lonely life and most of the responsibilities of the family are left to the wives.

Today, baseball is more family friendly than in the past. In my era, especially at the beginning of my career, it was rare that you were allowed to miss a game for the birth of your child. Fortunately, things have changed for the better and family life is now a priority.

Baseball life can be a challenge for many reasons. Phoebe never complained about it and she always supported me and my career. It was hard for her. She'd make plans for us to go out to dinner after a Sunday afternoon game at Fenway, but if I had a bad day I'd be in a miserable mood and want to cancel. I wasn't a happy-go-lucky guy during the season. I just couldn't leave the game at the ballpark. I'd see other players who were able to do that, and I used to be jealous of them. Fred Lynn was a great example; nothing seemed to bother him. Everything bothered me. All those years while I was playing, Phoebe tolerated a lot of crap from me. She deserves a gold star.

I don't know what else to say about her except she's the best person I know and that she provides the strength for all of us. She's a wonderful mother, and a wonderful grandmother. You can ask anyone in our family and they will tell you the exact same thing. I don't know what I'd do without her. She's been with me through all the highs and the lows. She's been through the cancer, through the depression, through our son's ordeal, which absolutely crushed her. She's still here and she always manages to have a bright outlook on things. Phoebe has been through some things that could have knocked her out of the game, but she's a very strong woman. She's really been the backbone of our family.

Some of the things you think about when you're doing a book about your life includes thinking back on your childhood. My mother worked at my uncle's dance studio, so it was impossible for me to avoid dancing. I was a tap dancer until I was 14 years old and I would participate in the annual dance recital. I really believe that dancing is the reason I had quick feet. Think about tap dancing and the discipline needed to become a tap dancer and tell me that doesn't affect your agility in a positive way. It's what gave me my quickness, my speed. Maybe at the time I did it reluctantly, but, boy, am I glad that I tapped! And every now and then, even though I've had 11 procedures on my left knee, I feel the urge to start tap dancing in the booth.

When I came to Boston from the Angels, one of the most difficult adjustments was the fact that my parents were able to come to Fenway and see me play. Believe me, there are good things about your parents watching you play major league baseball, but it was also stressful. They would come up on most of the weekends. It was awful standing out on the field and being booed, or worse, while your parents were sitting in the stands. It's a horrible feeling.

So, it's kind of weird, but since I've been a broadcaster, over the years, I've become a totally different person. I don't bring the game home with me the way I did as a player. I think I've been a much better husband, an all-around better person, because, now, I'm much more laid-back.

I guess my biggest regret is I could never really enjoy my time as a player because I never felt comfortable. Even when I was doing well, I was always expecting the next shoe to drop and blow everything up. That's just the way I was; that was my mentality. However, I believe that type of attitude made me, in many ways, persevere in life.

I think I'm more popular now than I was as a player. When you're on television, and I've been on it now going into my 32nd year, you establish yourself, people feel as if you're part of their family. They feel like they know you personally. It's incredible having people say that they remember a particular call or play, or that they missed me on TV when I couldn't work. The feedback you get from the fans is remarkable.

I'm not saying I wasn't popular as a player. I was a local kid who did well with the Red Sox. Not a Hall of Fame player, but good enough to be an All-Star, and to be inducted into the Red Sox Hall of Fame. I was never really heckled or picked on by the Red Sox fans. I think I was well liked. But my popularity as a broadcaster is 10 times the amount it was as a player.

It's just a shame that I had so many injuries. I played in the days before we had the technology that they have today. The first time I hurt my knee was at Yankee Stadium in 1979. I made a terrible base running play. I led the game off with a triple. Catfish Hunter was pitching on one of those hot New York days. Rick Burleson hit a little popup down the first base line. I was under the impression that Yankees first baseman Chris Chambliss was going to catch the ball going away from home plate. There were no outs in the inning. Instead, Willie Randolph made the play and threw me out at home plate by about 10 feet. As I went in to slide, my spike got caught. My body went one way, but my knee went in another direction. It was just a horrible play on my part.

I honestly believe, to this day, that I played the remainder of the year with torn cartilage in my left knee that was suffering more damage as I continued to play. My knee problem became a constant issue. Every year I'd have to go in and get a "clean up." Eventually that's what ended my career, possibly, a few years before it should have ended. I just couldn't do it anymore.

When I reported to spring training in 1986, I knew I was done. For the last couple of years, I noticed a difference in my speed. I was getting thrown out by half a step on balls that I use to beat out in the infield. There were plays at second base, where I was able to dive and make a play, now I'd dive but I couldn't quite get there. As time went on, I became more aware of these changes. It was frustrating because speed was really my game. Speed gave me the range that I had; it gave me the ability to steal bases. With every knee injury, I could just sense my career slipping away.

In May of 1980, one of my worst injuries occurred in a game at Cleveland Stadium, when I had to play right field in the eighth inning. Fred Lynn was hurt that day. Don Zimmer got into a situation where he was pinch-hitting for Dwight Evans and needed a right fielder. Zim looked down the bench and asked if any of us could play right field. No one said anything. So, I volunteered. In the bottom of the eighth inning, I moved from second base to right field and Jack Brohammer, who had pinch-hit for Dwight, went to second base.

Of course, the first pitch Bob Stanley threw Indians catcher Ron Hassey was hit up in the air to right field. I looked like an absolute idiot trying to make a play on a routine fly ball. I went back, I came in. Again, I went back, I came in. Eventually my knee gave way; the ball landed behind me and the runner ended up at third base. It was probably the most embarrassing moment in my baseball career.

People ask me how long I'm going to broadcast. Quite frankly, except during the time after my son's incident, retirement has never entered my mind. I have no desire to retire. Although I'm not a kid anymore, I'm 66 years old, I still get a rush when the umpire says, "Play ball!"

I can't say I have an age in mind at which point I would consider retirement. My performance and my health will determine when it's time to leave.

One thing I'll never forget was the Red Sox and NESN honoring me on August 20, 2017, for my 30th year in broadcasting. When they host a celebration, they do it up right! They asked me who I wanted to have attend the ceremony, if they needed to fly anyone in for the event. I said I wanted to do something a little different. I really wanted my family and my doctors from Mass General Hospital with me on the field.

I brought out all the doctors who have worked with me, the ones who have kept me alive for the last 10 years. It was kind of funny for me to see them in a different atmosphere as opposed to at the hospital in their white coats. On this day, they were just fans having a great time. It was an honor for me to have them on the field with me, because without these people, I wouldn't be here today.

I didn't want to make it a huge production. I wanted it to be just my family, my grandchildren, and my doctors. My producer, Mike Narracci, was also on the field. We've worked together for such a long time and I wanted him there. Then there were members of the Red Sox organization and NESN, for example, Sam Kennedy,

It was a real honor to walk on the field at Fenway Park in 2017 to celebrate my 30 years in the Red Sox booth. (Getty Images)

a terrific guy and friend; chairman Tom Werner; Linda Pizzutti Henry; Sean McGrail; and others.

They've all been great to me.

Dr. Walter O'Donnell is my pulmonologist. Dr. Alice Shaw is my oncologist. Dr. Henning Willers is my radiologist/oncologist. Dr. Cameron Wright is my surgeon. Dr. Joanne Shepherd does my biopsies and specializes in nuclear medicine. Dr. Jerrold Rosembaum is my psychiatrist. Dr. Larry Ronan could not be there that day, but I owe him my life. As my primary care physician, he's the one who first detected an abnormality in my chest X-ray and I am eternally grateful to him.

A funny story: Dr. Wright is a thoracic surgeon. He's a real straightforward, no-nonsense type of guy. But when all the doctors were lined up in the dugout prior to going out onto the field that day, John Farrell came walking by and Dr. Wright yelled out, "Let's go, Sox!" Of course, Farrell didn't respond because there were thousands of people in the stands. I looked at Dr. Wright and he's shaking his head, as if wondering, why did I say that?

It's almost like everyone goes to the ballpark and becomes a kid!

I also want to mention my sister, Judy. She's one of my biggest fans. A great Red Sox fan. She's five years my junior, and even when she moved to Florida to be close to our parents, she never stopped supporting me. She has stuck with me throughout all my ordeals. She lost her husband way too young, to lung cancer, but she's strong and resilient. Judy has been an amazing source of love and support since we were kids.

My other two children, Jordan and Jenna, have also endured the immense pain of what happened with Jared. They both loved and miss Jen. The situation has been so difficult for them. Jordan, recently married, has moved out of state. Jenna and her husband have stayed in the area. As a parent, it's good to see them find some happiness and be able to move on with their lives.

The last decade or so of my life has been a challenge, but the love and support that I've received from my family and friends has been something I will never, ever forget.

Thanks to all of the fans who have been there for me through thick and thin. You'll never know how much you've helped me get through some of the darkest times of my life. I just want to be the most insightful and entertaining analyst I can be for you on Red Sox broadcasts.

You've welcomed me into your living rooms, family rooms, TV rooms, man caves, wherever you watch Red Sox games, for more than 30 years. I hope that continues for many years to come.

AFTERWORD

I had first met Jerry Remy when I was an intern for Joe Castiglione and Ken Coleman back in 1989, and then Joe and Bob Starr in 1990. I was in the booth next door and Jerry had this obsession with the lineup, and getting it at, like 2:30 in the afternoon for a 7:00 PM game. He would come to me and say, "You got a lineup yet?" So, that's how I first got to know him.

I spent the next 10 seasons in the minor leagues, broadcasting games on radio, and my last year was with the Pawtucket Red Sox. I worked at three different levels of the minor leagues, from Single-A to Triple-A.

I was kind of at a crossroads in my career, really, as to what I was going to do. I was turning 30 and didn't really know if I was taking the right route to the big leagues. During the 2000 season, I went with the PawSox staff to a day/night doubleheader against Cleveland at Fenway. I knew at this time Bob Kurtz would not be returning to NESN. I ended up in the booth sitting on the stairs behind Jerry in between games. Jerry turned to me and said, "Are you interested in coming up here?" I said, "Yes!" I told him I'd been in the minors for 10 years and my goal was to get up to the majors. Jerry Remy, along with Dan Duquette, who was the general manager at the time, were very instrumental in getting me to the major leagues, and to Boston.

The next step was trying to figure out what the heck I was doing. I had done years in the minor leagues but I was still very green when it came to the major leagues. There's such a big difference between broadcasting in the minor leagues and broadcasting in the majors. And you really need a veteran, much like a player who needs a veteran when they arrive to kind of take him under his wing, and Jerry really did that for me.

I'm talking about everything, from the baseball side of things to where to sit on the charter, where to sit on the bus, how to get into the stadiums, how to get into the booths. And the TV stuff. I had no idea what I was doing television-wise, and really leaned on him a great deal for, not only his expert analysis, but really, just how to do TV and get used to having five people talking to you in your ear while you're broadcasting. Jerry was huge in really helping me get through that process.

We have been through so much together over the years, especially when he came back after the first bout of cancer and the depression. I think it was uncomfortable for him, and there were a lot of times when I think he questioned whether he could do it. That's when we really became friends, and that was like, our ninth year of working together, and then he became part of my inner circle, and has been ever since, even though I've been gone for years.

It was that year when we really started to get into our antics. We had been doing funny things and having funny conversations, like two guys in a bar, on the team plane. We'd crack each other up. So we shifted that unscripted stuff into the booth. It wasn't forced or premeditated. It just kind of happened. We would just react to things as they occurred. It happened organically like two friends having a conversation.

There were a few that were embarrassing, like the joke was on me. Very early in my career, I'd say like 2002—it was around the lunar eclipse—and it was supposed to be that night, and we were talking about it on the air, and I started talking about it, and referencing what I thought took place during a lunar eclipse. The more I talked, the more obvious it became that I really didn't know anything about it; in my scenario, the sun kind of crosses in front of the moon, and we'd all be fried and dead. That one had a lot of traction and Jerry just played along. That was really the first one with Jerry, but there were just so many over the years. My personal favorite, because it just was so surprising, was Jerry's tooth falling out in between us on the table in the middle of a play. I ended up putting it back in his mouth, and I took out a hammer and some tools from a tool box we had in the booth. I ended up getting an honorary doctorate from the New England Dentistry Association, and I was invited to their yearly conference. So, thanks to Jerry, I am now a dentist.

People talk about the boob grab, which was another incident that just came out of nowhere. There was this guy and girl, actually two couples who were sitting in the bleachers. Mike Narracci, our director, kept the camera on them, and Jerry says, "Isn't this nice? You know, a lovely summer evening to be out on a romantic night." One problem: while we were still on camera with these couples, a guy reaches over and grabs her left boob. We just couldn't speak. Our laughter was to the point where we couldn't get words out of our mouths. I think Nick Markakis was up and I tried to do the Markakis at-bat. I couldn't. Part of the laughter was what people couldn't hear back home. Narracci said in my earpiece, "I'm all done, I stayed on them too long, I'm finished." I went on the talkback to him, and I said, "Well, look at it this way, at least you can direct porn if they fire you." There was a lot of giggling between Jerry and I about things that were coming from the truck that fans at home couldn't tell. There were so many, it was unbelievable. It was fun for us.

In my last five years, we had three last-place finishes. There was a championship mixed in there in '13, but we had some bad baseball for a lot of those years. There were times when the games weren't competitive, so we got off on tangents on things that had nothing to do with the game. I think there were some people who thought it should be all balls and strikes, and that we shouldn't have fun and they just wanted to listen to the game, and see the game, and they didn't need all of that other stuff. We had decided that we were going to do it the way we were doing it until somebody told us otherwise.

We did have serious baseball conversations as well. To me, one of Jerry's strengths was that he thought like a manager, in that he first-guesses a lot and is right a lot. Jerry gets out there ahead of the play and throws his knowledge out there early. Hit-and-runs, possible scenarios, squeezes. He's thinking along like a manager would be. Even the next inning, as to who's coming up, what's the scenario. So, that makes him special, it really does, and he's very, very good at it.

I think Jerry brought out the best in me. Jerry was my first major league partner and I'm so glad I got to learn from him. He was so good at breaking down the inside stuff of the game both on and off the field. He taught me so much about TV and being comfortable with my game.

We called the 2004 season almost in its entirety. The first World Series in 86 years. That was big for both of us. We could see it building and building and we knew what we were going through was special. And it was a loose team with a lot of characters and that made all of it so much fun and pleasurable as broadcasters.

Then there were those tough times with Jerry. There was a lot there that we were dealing with, and to be honest, you're with your partners in the big leagues many more hours than you are with your wife or family. You get there every day at 2:30 PM and you leave at 10:30, and you're together all that time on the plane, and in the hotels, on off days, and you really spend every day with that person, so it's like a marriage in some ways.

There were games when he was going through depression that Jerry was really quiet. I knew he was struggling. And there were times where I basically would just pick it up and go, and I don't want to say cover for him, because he always made it, but there were some innings, middle innings of games, where sometimes you could just tell he was going into kind of a shell or a haze, whatever it was. It kind of overtook him. That happened from time to time, especially leading up to when he left the first time, '09.

Then there was the time when the depression and anxiety affected him out of the booth. We were in Cleveland and when I came into the lobby and he was sitting down there, and he said, "I don't wanna go."

And I said, "Okay, well, what are you afraid of?"

And he pointed toward the doors at the Marriott and he said, "All that out there."

I said, "All right, we'll just sit here." I sat with him for about 25 minutes, and then I said, "Well, why don't we go over to the park and if we get there and you're just not feeling any better, then we can come right back."

And he's like, "Okay, I'll try." We got to the park and he got through that game. That night we flew to Tampa, I guess that morning is when he called Phoebe to come get him. So, it had reached its lowest point. I did not see Jerry for a month after that.

Regardless, Jerry is the strongest person I know. He has been open and honest about his struggles and overcome every one. He does not give up and has been a true friend to me over the years. When I learned in August of 2015 that I would not be returning for the 2016 season with the Red Sox, it was very difficult news. We found out our partnership was coming to an end after 15 years. When word got out during a game in Chicago and the writers began to gather outside the booth in the ninth inning, Jerry intervened on my behalf, so I could leave without comment. I still had to finish out the last six weeks of the season, and he helped me through my last 25 games and somehow got me through my last game and public farewell. For that I will be eternally grateful.

Through it all, we've been there for each other every step of the way. Jerry and I were close and remain so to this day, even though I've moved on and now broadcast San Diego Padres games and live across the country.

We talk often about everything. I will always support him and be in his corner because I know he's done the same for me. I couldn't be prouder of him. He's a great example of someone who never gives up. He's my friend. And I'll always cherish that.

Don Orsillo was the television voice of the Boston Red Sox on NESN from 2001 to 2015. He is currently the play-by-play announcer for the San Diego Padres on Fox Sports San Diego.

IN TRIBUTE TO
NICK CAFARDO

Obviously, we were shocked by the horrible news that Nick Cafardo had passed away on February 20, 2019, during Red Sox spring training in Fort Myers, Florida.

The day before Nick passed, he and I were talking on the phone about the book you're currently reading. He sounded fine, totally normal, and his spirits were up. I was still at home at that time, but I was looking forward to seeing him when I got down to Florida.

Pam Kenn, the Red Sox's vice president of community, alumni, and player relations, called me the following day and gave me the news. Nick had apparently suffered an embolism at JetBlue Park, and despite the Red Sox medical team's best efforts, they were unable to revive him. Pam knew Nick and I were working on this book together, and she didn't want me to hear about it second-hand. I was just in total shock and disbelief.

Because I was still up in Massachusetts, I was able to attend Nick's wake and give my condolences to his family. I felt so terrible for his wife, Leanne; his daughter, Emilee; and his son, Ben, who followed his dad into the sports world and works at ESPN. It was very, very tough for all of us to accept what had happened.

Nick was incredibly respected by the baseball community. During his many years in the business, he had become someone who was known and liked nationally, not just in Boston. It wasn't just other people in the media who admired him, either. Nick had the confidence of players, coaches, and managers, who knew he could be trusted with any kind of information. He probably had more contacts around the league than anyone I know. That's part of the reason he was able to write that great Sunday column for the *Boston Globe*.

I had known Nick for a long, long time. He started covering the Red Sox for the *Patriot Ledger* in the 1980s, and then reported on them and the Patriots for the *Globe* starting in 1989. But it wasn't until the last couple of years, when we started working on this book together, that our acquaintance developed into a friendship.

It's so sad to see that this book has come out without him here to enjoy it, but hopefully it serves as a tribute to him.

—Jerry Remy